THE RESTORATION OF A SINNER

David's Heart Revealed

JOHN MACARTHUR

THOMAS NELSON
Since 1798

Published in Nashville, Tennessee, by Thomas Nelson. Thomas Nelson is a trademark of Thomas Nelson, Inc.

Published in association with the literary agency of Wolgemuth & Associates, Inc.

Layout, design, and writing assistance by Gregory C. Benoit Publishing, Old Mystic, CT. GᴛB

Thomas Nelson, Inc. titles may be purchased in bulk for educational, business, fund-raising, or sales promotional use. For information, please e-mail *SpecialMarkets@ThomasNelson.com*.

ISBN 978-1-4185-3405-9

Printed in the United States of America

13 14 15 QG 10 9 8

CONTENTS

~ ~

Israel in the Time of David

34°30' 35° 35°30' 36°

Sidon

Damascus
33°30'

Tyre

Dan

Kedesh

33° Exact location questionable Hazor 33°

? Acco

0 10 20
Scale of Miles

Galilee Sea of Galilee **Bashan**

Golan? Ashtaroth

R. Yarmuk

Jokneam En Dor Edrei

Dor Megiddo Shunem

Ramoth

32°30' **The Great Sea** Ibleam Beth Shean 32°30'

Gilead

Tirzah

Zaphon

Shechem R. Jabbok
Succoth

Aphek Tappuah Shiloh **Ammon**

Joppa

32° Rabbah 32°

Jabneel Bethel Ai Gilgal
Gezer Aijalon Gibeon
Ekron Timnah Kirjath Gibeah Jericho
Jearim Jerusalem Heshbon Bezer?
Ashdod Makkedah Beth Shemesh
Gath Jarmuth Bethlehem Medeba
Ashkelon Azekah

Adullam
Philistia Mareshah Hebron
Gaza Lachish Dibon
Debir The Salt Aroer 31°30'
En Gedi Sea R. Arnon

Moab

34°30' Beersheba 35° 35°30' 36°

(FOR MORE DETAIL, SEE THE MAP ON PAGE 34.)

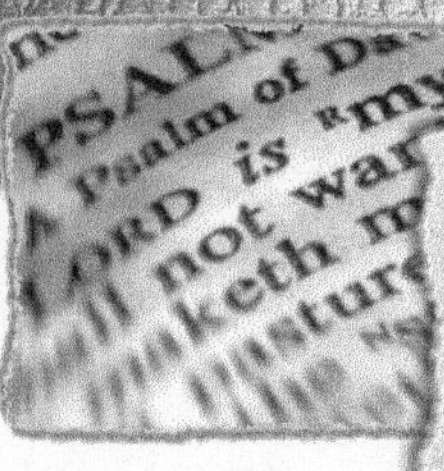

Introduction

Saul was Israel's first king, but he was not faithful to the Lord, and thus was not faithful to the Lord's people. When he refused to repent, God rejected him and chose a new king for Israel. This new king provided hope for his people, because he was unlike Saul. The Lord Himself said, "I have found . . . a man after My own heart, who will do all My will" (Acts 13:22). That man was David, and while he would be Israel's second king, he would be the first king to follow after God's own heart.

Yet David was also a great sinner; it wasn't long after he became king that he committed both adultery and murder. This raises the obvious question: how can an adulterous murderer be called a man after God's own heart? This is the great question of David's life and, of course, of every Christian's life as well. How can an ungodly person (as we all are) be seen by God as faithful? This study sets out to answer that very question.

As you work through this study guide, you will meet a variety of memorable characters. You will encounter Joab, the leader of Israel's army, who was both a shrewd military general and a treacherous assassin. You will get to know Mephibosheth, Saul's grandson, who was lame in both feet—and Ziba, his shady steward. You will witness the terrible pain within David's household, as three of his sons die tragically. And, of course, you will get to know King David.

In these twelve studies, we will jump back and forth in history, looking at one historical period and then skipping forward or backward in time as needed. We will examine the nature of sin and the importance of repentance, and we will learn the value of obedience. But through it all, we will also learn precious truths about the character of God, and we will see His great faithfulness in keeping His promises. As we view God's faithfulness toward His servants in this study—and expect the same from Him today, in our own lives—we will ultimately learn what it means to be a person after God's own heart.

What We'll Be Studying

This study guide is divided into four distinct sections in which we will examine selected Bible passages:

Section 1: History. In this first section, we will focus on the historical setting of our Bible text. These five lessons will give a broad overview of the people, places, and events that are important to this study. They will also provide the background for the next two sections. This is our most purely historical segment, focusing simply on what happened and why.

SECTION 2: CHARACTERS. The four lessons in this section will give us an opportunity to zoom in on the characters from our Scripture passages. Some of these people were introduced in section 1, but in this part of the study guide we will take a much closer look at these personalities. Why did God see fit to include them in His Book in the first place? What made them unique? What can we learn from their lives? In this practical section, we will answer all of these questions and more, as we learn how to live wisely by emulating the wisdom of those who came before us.

SECTION 3: THEMES. Section 3 consists of two lessons in which we will consider some of the broader themes and doctrines touched on in our selected Scripture passages. This is the guide's most abstract portion, wherein we will ponder specific doctrinal and theological questions that are important to the church today. As we ask what these truths mean to us as Christians, we will also look for practical ways to base our lives upon God's truth.

SECTION 4: SUMMARY AND REVIEW. In our final section, we will look back at the principles we have discovered in the scriptures throughout this study guide. These will be our "takeaway" principles, those which permeate the Bible passages that we have studied. As always, we will be looking for ways to make these truths a part of our everyday lives.

⌁ ABOUT THE LESSONS ⌁

⊰ Each study begins with an introduction that provides the background for the selected Scripture passages.

⊰ To assist you in your reading, a section of notes—a miniature Bible commentary of sorts—offers both cultural information and additional insights.

⊰ A series of questions is provided to help you dig a bit deeper into the Bible text.

⊰ Overriding principles brought to light by the Bible text will be studied in each lesson. These principles summarize a variety of doctrines and practical truths found throughout the Bible.

⊰ Finally, additional questions will help you mine the deep riches of God's Word and, most importantly, to apply those truths to your own life.

Section 1:

History

In This Section:

UNITING A DIVIDED HOUSE

2 SAMUEL 2, 5

∼ HISTORICAL BACKGROUND ∼

Israel had been led for hundreds of years by judges (judges were individuals called by God to lead His people against their enemies, to settle disputes, and to protect the nation). But the Israelites eventually decided that they no longer wanted judges to lead them. Under the judges, the people were dependent on God to determine when a judge was necessary. Now instead of relying on God to protect them, the Israelites wanted to imitate the world around them. All the nations of Canaan were governed by kings, so Israel wanted a king as well.

Samuel, Israel's last judge and one of God's great prophets, warned the people that exchanging the Lord for a monarchy was a destructive idea—a king would harm the people with taxes, and would exploit them for his own gain. Yet the people refused to listen, so the Lord instructed Samuel to anoint a young man named Saul as Israel's first king.

Sadly, Samuel's words of warning were fulfilled. Saul was disobedient to God, and the Lord eventually rejected him as king. So the Lord chose another man whom—unlike Saul—had his heart turned to obedience. His name was David, and Samuel anointed him as Israel's next king. Saul, however, continued to reign for many years. But he didn't reign well. Knowing that God had rejected him in favor of David, Saul spent the remainder of his life trying to kill David. Tragically, Saul died in battle against the Philistines, and all his sons died with him—all except one, a man named Ishbosheth.

This study opens shortly after Saul's death, when David is preparing to take over the kingship. But Saul's sole survivor, Ishbosheth, feels that the throne is his by birthright, and the nation is divided in its loyalties.

COMPETITION FOR THE THRONE: *Saul's only remaining son raises himself up as heir to Saul's throne, effectively dividing the nation of Israel into two factions.*

8. ABNER: Abner was King Saul's cousin, and the leader of the Israelite army. He remained loyal to Saul's house, even though David had already been anointed by God to be the next king. His loyalty was misplaced at this point, but he eventually would agree to serve David as faithfully as he had Saul.

ISHBOSHETH: This was Saul's only surviving son; the others had all been killed in Saul's last battle against the Philistines. His name means "man of shame."

9. KING OVER GILEAD: The areas listed in this verse under Ishbosheth's reign include most of Israel.

10. THE HOUSE OF JUDAH: David's family was from Judah, one of the twelve tribes of Israel. This tribe would remain loyal to David throughout his kingship and beyond. Eventually, the nation of Israel would split into two separate nations: Israel and Judah.

13. JOAB: Joab was David's nephew and the leader of his army. We will look at him more closely in a later study.

THE TRAGEDY OF CIVIL WAR: *Two great generals, Abner and Joab, attempt to prevent all-out warfare, but it proves unavoidable.*

14. LET THE YOUNG MEN NOW ARISE: Abner proposed a combat of champions, twelve from each side, rather than a full-scale war. This was a sensible suggestion insofar as it went—the outcome of the combat, had it been decisive, would have prevented civil war where brother was killing brother. The problem, however, was that Abner and the men of Israel should have submitted to the kingship of David, since he was the man God had anointed to sit on the throne over all Israel. Abner's plan failed, and the civil war erupted despite his suggestion.

18. THE THREE SONS OF ZERUIAH: Zeruiah was David's sister and the mother of Joab.

19. ASAHEL PURSUED ABNER: Asahel was Joab's brother, and in this tragic story he showed himself to be a man of character and determination. He was pursuing Abner in battle, and to have killed the general of the opposing side would have immediately ended the entire conflict (and also brought him great honor). Asahel was clearly out of his league fighting Abner, as will be seen, yet he refused to turn aside from the pursuit. He is reminiscent of David, who did not hesitate to face the giant Goliath in a single combat that brought great victory to God's people.

22. Turn aside from following me: Abner also showed himself to be a man of character in this sad episode. He did not want to kill a young man of Asahel's quality, so he tried repeatedly to dissuade him from battle. But the seeds of division were already sown. Division is the work of the devil, and when God's people are divided against one another, only tragedy can result. Rather than fighting the enemy of our souls, godly men and women attack one another. In doing so, they waste their efforts, just as Abner and Asahel did, fighting against each other rather than against the Philistines.

23. died on the spot: This terrible tragedy would have equally terrible long-term consequences. Joab never forgave Abner for killing his brother, even though it was done in battle. We will see the results in a later study.

25. the children of Benjamin: One of the twelve tribes of Israel. It was also Saul's tribe, and they had remained steadfastly loyal to him throughout his turbulent reign.

26. Shall the sword devour forever? : Abner was responsible for the conflict in the first place, since he led the men of Israel into battle.

3:1. there was a long war between the house of Saul and the house of David: Many tribes of Israel continued to support the house of Saul, rather than submitting to David as their king. The Lord had publicly anointed him and told the people, through Samuel, that he was God's selected ruler—yet David still had to establish his throne by force.

⌁ Reading 2 Samuel 5:1–12 ⌁

The Kingdom Is United: *Abner changes sides and comes to serve David, and the nation of Israel submits to his kingship. Soon after, David establishes himself in Jerusalem.*

1. Then all the tribes of Israel came to David: Several years had passed since the battle of chapter 2, and much had happened. Abner had abandoned Ishbosheth and joined forces with David. Before any good could come from that alliance, however, Joab took revenge for the death of Asahel by murdering Abner. Sometime after these events, Ishbosheth was murdered by two of his captains.

2. you were the one who led Israel: King Saul had tried repeatedly to murder David, after Samuel anointed David as king. During those years, David had led a small band of fighting men on many raids and excursions against the Philistines, and the people of Israel had celebrated his victories in songs.

4. David was thirty years old when he began to reign: David had begun his career as a leader in Israel when he was just a teenager, on the day he stepped forward and slew Goliath. Yet he was forced to endure more than ten years of hardship, resistance, and fighting before he could finally ascend to the throne in relative security.

6. Jebusites: The Jebusites were one of the Canaanite nations that Israel had been commanded to drive out of the promised land (Exodus 23:23), yet they were still living there and still causing problems for Israel. They had traditionally occupied the city of Jerusalem, which they called Jebus.

the blind and the lame will repel you: The Jebusites placed their faith in the fortification and security of their city, a mind-set that is as common as it is foolish. God's people must never fall into the trap of thinking that military might or financial security will stave off ruin. As the Jebusites would soon discover, God's hand is not stopped by man's fortifications.

7. Zion: This is the first appearance in Scripture of the name *Zion*. It originally referred specifically to the Jebusite stronghold, which became the City of David after this battle, but Scripture uses it to refer to Jerusalem in general, the earthly City of God.

8. water shaft: A secret tunnel ran from the city down to the spring of Gihon. It was intended to provide water if the city were ever under siege and was one of the defenses that gave the Jebusites their false sense of security. Ironically, David used that very "defense" against the people, as his men climbed up the water shaft and took the city from the inside.

12. the Lord had established him: This was the foundation of David's great leadership in Israel: he always remembered that it was the Lord who had raised him from a humble shepherd to the king of God's people. Saul lost sight of that fact and became proud and stubborn, but David always remembered that he was subject to the Lord's will, an attitude that carried him even through periods of sin and heartbreak.

↬ First Impressions ↫

1. *Why did the people of Israel try to make Ishbosheth king instead of David? Why did Abner, Saul's great military leader, side against David?*

2. Why did Abner suggest holding a "contest of champions" rather than open battle? Was this a good idea, in your opinion? Why did it fail?

3. Was Abner justified when he killed Asahel? Was Asahel wise or unwise to keep pursuing him?

4. *Why were the Jebusites so arrogant in their response to David? How was their faith misplaced?*

↜ Some Key Principles ↝

Division is the devil's tool.

The nation of Israel divided when King Saul died, each half placing their allegiance behind a different heir to the throne. That same division would return later in David's reign, and would ultimately divide Israel into two separate nations. Each time the people were divided, strife and civil war resulted. Abner was forced to fight Asahel, a young man he admired, when the two men should have been fighting side by side against the Philistines.

This is Satan's goal in dividing God's people: if we are busy contending against one another, we won't be doing battle against the forces of darkness. The evil one loves to see Christians bickering and scratching at one another, and he will do all he can to cause division and contention within the church.

The Lord wants His people to be unified together in one body, focused on serving one another and caring for one another as members of the same body. "Now I plead with you, brethren," wrote the apostle Paul, "by the name of our Lord Jesus Christ, that you all speak the same thing, and that there be no divisions among you, but that you be perfectly joined together in the same mind and in the same judgment.... For where there are envy, strife, and divisions among you, are you not carnal and behaving like mere men? For when one says, 'I am of Paul,' and another, 'I am of Apollos,' are you not carnal?" (1 Corinthians 1:10; 3:3–4).

Submit to the Lord's chosen leaders.

The division within Israel came about because some were unwilling to submit themselves to David's authority. They felt that a son of Saul should be the next king, and they set about making it a reality—in spite of the fact that God had publicly proclaimed David king through the anointing of Samuel.

The basic mind-set of the Israelites was that they knew who should govern better than God knew. They thought they had the right to choose their own rulers—but this was actually not true. The Lord is the one who places people in positions of power and authority, and He expects His people to submit themselves to those authorities.

God's Word calls us to be submissive to those in authority, whether in government, at home, in the church, or at the workplace. The Bible says, "Let every soul be subject to the governing authorities. For there is no authority except from God, and the authorities that exist are appointed by God. Therefore whoever resists the authority resists the ordinance of God, and those who resist will bring judgment on themselves" (Romans 13:1–2).

God's people are established by God, not by our own might.

David had to fight to establish his throne in Israel. He faced much opposition, both from outside enemies, such as the Philistines, and from foes within his own nation. He fought boldly and effectively, and eventually he gained victory over those foes—yet he declared clearly that his throne had been established, not by the power of his mighty sword but by the power and will of God Himself.

Conversely, the Jebusites placed their faith in their own might. The city of Jerusalem was nearly impregnable, because of both geography and man-made fortifications, and it could stand strong even under a lengthy siege. The Jebusites were convinced that they had made themselves secure, and they saw no need to fear God or His people. Yet the Lord eventually used their own might against them.

We do not find our security or success through our own efforts or through the world around us. It is the Lord who establishes us where He wants us, "Not by might nor by power, but by My Spirit,' says the LORD of hosts" (Zechariah 4:6). We attain success and security by submitting to His sovereign hand.

5.   How might this civil war have been avoided? What did the war cost the nation of Israel?

6.   What motivated the people of Israel to reject David as king? What was wrong with their thinking?

7. When have you witnessed division among God's people? What caused it? What was the result?

8. Are you promoting peace and unity, or stirring up strife and division? In what areas might the Lord be calling you to be a peacemaker?

ᴖ TAKING IT PERSONALLY ᴖ

9. Where do you find security? Do you place your faith in your own efforts, or in God's sovereignty?

10. How well do you submit to those in authority in government? at work? at church? at home?

A THRONE ESTABLISHED FOREVER

2 SAMUEL 7

↱ HISTORICAL BACKGROUND ↰

Most of David's kingship was characterized by conflict and warfare. Israel had many enemies who persisted in trying to conquer her—some even wanted to wipe her off the map. The Philistines were one of their most dangerous enemies, and David spent most of his reign overthrowing their tyranny. In addition to foreign enemies, David also faced multiple rebellions from the Israelites themselves, and even one of his own sons briefly overthrew him from power.

Despite this opposition, David never lost sight of the fact that all of his blessings were from God, and he longed to do something to demonstrate his love and gratitude for the Lord. In this frame of mind, David got the idea of building a beautiful temple in which the people of Israel could worship God.

The Lord had commanded Moses and Aaron to construct a portable tabernacle during their exodus from Egypt. This structure was made of cloth and animal skins, designed to be set up and taken down easily as the people moved from place to place in the wilderness. The tabernacle housed the ark of the covenant, which was the nation's symbol of God's presence, and the tabernacle itself was the figurative "dwelling place" of God among His people.

But now, with Israel's wilderness wanderings long since completed, David felt that it was not right that he should live in a beautiful palace while God continued to dwell in a portable tent, so he devised a plan to build the temple. The idea itself was not wrong; God would indeed lead another king to build a temple—but not David. Nevertheless, the Lord blessed David immensely for the love behind his desire to build a permanent dwelling place for the Almighty.

A Dwelling Place for God: *Later in David's life, he reflects on the fact that he lives in a palace, while God's tabernacle is merely a tent. He decides to rectify that.*

1. the Lord had given him rest from all his enemies: This passage probably takes place much later in David's reign, near the end of his life. The ark of the covenant had been residing in Kirjath Jearim (see the map in the Introduction) for many years, and David had finally returned it to the temple in Jerusalem where it belonged. (See 1 Samuel 4 and 2 Samuel 6 for further information.)

2. the ark of God dwells inside tent curtains: The ark of the covenant was an article of sacred furniture that God had commanded the people to build during their exodus from Egypt. It was an ornate gold-covered chest with two golden sculptures of angels on the top, and inside it contained important artifacts from Israel's trip out of slavery. Its special importance in the people's worship was that it symbolized the presence of God among His people. Its proper place was inside the Holiest of Holies in the tabernacle, separated from the rest of the tabernacle (and later, the temple) by thick, heavy curtains. David's concern was motivated by humility and gratitude: it didn't seem right that he should be living in a palace, placed there by God's gracious hand, while God Himself dwelt in a tent. David, of course, was not suggesting that the tabernacle or any other structure could contain the physical presence of God, but he was recognizing that the tabernacle represented God's presence with His people, and David wanted Him to be better represented.

3. Nathan: Nathan was a prophet who was closely associated with David as one of his advisors. He would later confront the king with a far less pleasant message, as we will see in Study 5.

do all that is in your heart: David's intentions were noble, and there was no question that the Lord had been with him in his reign—but apparently neither Nathan nor David consulted the Lord on these plans, an oversight that generally leads to errors. Fortunately, the Lord prevented David from doing anything amiss, but that's not always the case. It is important—and always wise—to seek God's counsel before undertaking any new plans.

God Speaks to Nathan: *David and Nathan had rushed forward in their plans without consulting God. Now God has His say in the matter.*

5. My servant David: The Lord's description of David as "My servant" indicated that David had made obedience to God a top priority in his life. He did not refer to King Saul, David's predecessor, in that way.

7. Wherever I have moved about with all the children of Israel: The Lord's presence had been with the people of Israel through their wilderness wanderings and into the promised land. As a symbol of His abiding presence, God had commanded the people to construct a movable tabernacle that could be assembled and disassembled as the nation moved from place to place.

8. I took you from the sheepfold: David was the youngest son of Jesse, and had spent his youth tending his father's sheep. Shepherding was one of the lowliest occupations in David's day, and his background would have been considered very humble. Yet the Lord had used David's experiences as a shepherd to prepare him for his kingship in many ways. He had single-handedly killed a lion and a bear, using the most rudimentary weapons—which set him in good stead to kill Goliath. He had also probably developed his skill as a musician and poet during those years, which enabled him to write many of the Psalms. Perhaps most important, however, was the very humbleness of his background, which helped him to remember that his position as king was due solely to the Lord's grace and kindness.

9. cut off all your enemies: David faced a great many enemies during his early years as king and the time prior to taking the throne. And the Lord had given him victory after victory over those who sought his destruction—but the process involved much shedding of blood. It was indeed the Lord's will that David defeat Israel's enemies, but He wanted His temple to be constructed by a man whose hands were not sullied with blood (1 Chronicles 22:7–8).

10. the sons of wickedness: The neighboring nations in Canaan had plagued Israel since they entered the promised land under Joshua's leadership. God had chosen David to subdue Israel's enemies, as well as to shepherd His people toward becoming a unified nation that was not divided by schisms and bids for power. David's job, then, was to unite and strengthen God's people—to care for them as he had once cared for his father's sheep. The job of building a permanent temple would fall to his descendants.

11. I commanded judges: Israel had been led for hundreds of years after entering the promised land by a series of judges that God had raised up. Eventually, however, the people had rebelled against that form of government, wanting to have a monarchy just like the nations around them. (For further study on that topic, see the previous book in this series, *Prophets, Priests, and Kings*.)

God Blesses David: The Lord now pronounces some profound blessings upon David and his descendants—and promises the coming Messiah.

12. I WILL ESTABLISH HIS KINGDOM: In the next few verses, the Lord made promises to David that had dual fulfillment: they were fulfilled in the short term through David's son Solomon, but they were (and will be) fulfilled in the larger, eternal sense through the Son of David, Jesus Christ. The ultimate realization of these promises is found only in Jesus, whose throne will literally be established forever.

14. HE SHALL BE MY SON: David could not have understood how this promise would be literally fulfilled in Jesus, the only begotten Son of God (Hebrews 1:5).

IF HE COMMITS INIQUITY: This portion of God's prophecy applied only to Solomon, not to Christ, "who committed no sin, nor was deceit found in His mouth" (1 Peter 2:22).

16. YOUR THRONE SHALL BE ESTABLISHED FOREVER: This promise was fulfilled in the person of Jesus Christ, of whom the apostle Luke wrote, "He will be great, and will be called the Son of the Highest; and the Lord God will give Him the throne of His father David. And He will reign over the house of Jacob forever, and of His kingdom there will be no end" (Luke 1:32–33).

DAVID'S THANKSGIVING: *After Nathan tells David what the Lord has said, the king goes straight to the tabernacle and bows before the Lord in humble adoration.*

18. WHO AM I: David demonstrated his humble heart in his response to the Lord's promises. He recognized his own humble origins as a shepherd, but he also understood that no man—regardless of birth or gifts or good deeds—has any right to expect grace and mercy from a holy God. David would later write, "What is man that You are mindful of him, and the son of man that You visit him?" (Psalm 8:4).

19. IS THIS THE MANNER OF MAN, O LORD GOD? : Another Bible translation renders this difficult phrase, "Is this your usual way of dealing with man, O Sovereign LORD?" (NIV).

21. TO MAKE YOUR SERVANT KNOW: David wisely recognized that the Lord shows His grace and love to men solely because He chooses to do so—no person has ever earned God's grace in any way. Today, as in David's time, God shows His true nature to mankind through His interventions of love, mercy, grace, and justice in order that all the world might learn of Him. He showered David with blessings both because He loved David and because He wanted the world around him to know that He alone is the one true God.

23. GOD WENT TO REDEEM: Here again, David's words had a depth of meaning that he could not have possibly realized. God would one day go forth Himself into the world in the person of Jesus Christ, specifically to redeem for Himself a holy nation. That nation would comprise far more than just the people of Israel, as God would make His redemption freely available to the entire human race.

28. Your words are true: David accepted by faith that God's words would come true. He had already learned that God always keeps His promises, no matter how impossible they may seem.

ᔑ First Impressions ᔐ

1. Why did David want to build a temple for God? What does this reveal about David's character?

2. What did David and Nathan do wrong in their decision to build a temple? What would have been a better approach to the idea?

3. *What did God promise to do for David?*

4. *What does David's prayer reveal about his attitude toward God's blessings? What does this reveal about his character? about God's character?*

↳ Some Key Principles ↲

God's covenants and promises are fulfilled in Jesus Christ.

The Lord made many promises to David, both concerning his own life and concerning the future of his kingdom. He promised that David's son would establish his throne and build a temple, and these promises were fulfilled in Solomon. The Lord also assured that His people would be planted in the promised land, no longer moving about from place to place, harassed by her former enemies—and these oaths were fulfilled in David's lifetime for the people of Israel.

But God's promises to David also went far beyond the lifetimes of himself and his son Solomon. He swore that He would establish David's throne and kingdom *forever*, not just for the lifetimes of men. The Lord also made covenants with others before David, such as Abraham and Noah, but those promises were only partially brought to completion in the lives of the patriarchs.

Jesus is the *complete* fulfillment of God's promises and covenants, because all human history has been leading up to God's final redemption of Adam's descendants, the eternal kingdom of God established and ruled over by His Son, Jesus Christ. Jesus is both Son of God and Son of Man, and His human ancestry is traced from the seed of David. David did see God's promises come to pass in his own life, true, but the final fulfillment will come in eternity through Christ.

The Lord makes His temple in people, not in buildings.

The pagan nations of David's day believed that a god looked favorably upon those who built the most costly temple in his honor. The more powerful the god, the more majestic the building. So what kind of god, according to such beliefs, would ever dwell inside a portable tent?

Yet this is precisely the form of tabernacle that the Lord commanded the Israelites to create during their exodus from Egypt. God was concerned not with lavish structures built in His honor but with obedient hearts molded by His Word. He selected David to be Israel's king because he had a heart for God, not because he would one day want to build a beautiful temple.

After Christ's resurrection and ascension, God sent His Holy Spirit to dwell in the hearts of His people, making *us* His tabernacles here on earth. As Jesus promised, "I will pray the Father, and He will give you another Helper, that He may abide with you forever— the Spirit of truth, whom the world cannot receive, because it neither sees Him nor knows Him; but you know Him, for He dwells with you and will be in you" (John 14:16–17). Each believer is now a living temple to God, and we are the most costly "structure" that could ever be dedicated to Him, since He paid for us with His own Son's blood.

God's dealings with mankind are through His grace, not man's merit.

Saul was king over Israel prior to David, but his entire reign was characterized by pride. He evidently felt that he somehow had merited being king, and that he could order events as he saw fit. This attitude led him into many grievous sins, including attempts to murder David and consulting a witch for guidance instead of God.

David's life, in contrast, was characterized by humility (with a few significant lapses, as we will see in Study 4). As a rule, he recognized that he had no merit in himself that deserved God's favor. God promised to establish his throne forever, and even brought the Messiah into the world through David's descendants—but David always understood that God did these things simply because He chose to, not because David had somehow earned His esteem.

God blesses His people because He loves us and it is His very nature to bless those whom He loves. God forgives us because He chooses to forgive, because His character is forgiving and gracious. No human being can ever earn God's blessings, and no person can ever make atonement for his sins. As Paul wrote, "For by grace you have been saved through faith, and that not of yourselves; it is the gift of God, not of works, lest anyone should boast" (Ephesians 2:8–9).

✎ Digging Deeper ✎

5. *Why did God not want David to build Him a temple? What does this reveal about God's character? about the kingdom of Christ?*

6. *How do God's promises to David apply to Christ? What elements of the promises were specifically referring to Him? What elements referred to Solomon and other kings?*

7. Why did God pour out such blessings on David—even though David and Nathan had failed to ask for His guidance concerning the temple? What does this reveal about God's character?

8. What is God's temple on earth today? Why did He choose such a "dwelling place"? What blessings does this bring to God's people?

9. List below some examples of God's grace that you have seen in your own life.

10. Take time right now to praise God for His blessings and grace in your life.

~ 3 ~
REMEMBERING PAST PROMISES

⤳ HISTORICAL BACKGROUND ⤵

In David's day, a king's authority was always under the threat of a coup. It seems there was always someone who felt he had a right to the throne, whether by birth or by virtue of some accomplishment, and the king had to be constantly on guard lest the usurper murder him or raise a rebellion against him.

It was not uncommon, therefore, for a king to ferret out any potential competitors and have them put to death. This was especially the case when the king had recently taken the throne—and doubly so if he had himself taken over the throne of another king—as David had. Monarchies were passed on from father to son in the ancient world, and Saul's throne would naturally have passed to his son Jonathan after his death. But God had rejected Saul as king and had anointed David in his place, so the proper heir to the throne was David rather than Saul's descendants. Nevertheless, there were those who thought otherwise—as we have already seen in Study 1.

In light of all of this, it would have been quite natural for David to want to search for any descendants of Saul who might pose a threat to his authority, and have them put to death—especially since he had already faced such a threat. And David did, in fact, search for Saul's descendants—but not to put them to death. He wanted to not only let them live but also to honor them and shower them with gifts.

In this chapter, we will discover how important it is to keep one's promises—and we will also see both mercy and grace in action.

LOOKING FOR WAYS TO BLESS: *David has established his throne, and now he searches out any descendants of Saul he can find—to bless them, not to gain revenge.*

1. DAVID SAID: In this chapter, we have gone back in time from our previous study to an earlier day in David's reign.

ANYONE WHO IS LEFT OF THE HOUSE OF SAUL: Saul, Israel's first king, had died by his own hand during a battle against the Philistines. Most of his sons had also died in battle that day, including Jonathan, whom Saul assumed would be his heir.

THAT I MAY SHOW HIM KINDNESS: This phrase might have startled David's listeners. Saul had tried repeatedly to murder David—even though David had always served him faithfully. Now that David had become king it would have been predictable for Saul's heirs to attempt to take back the throne—as we saw in Study 1. It was common practice, therefore, for a new king to hunt down anyone who might challenge his authority and have him overthrown. A Canaanite king might have asked, "Is there anyone left of my former enemy's household that I may put to death?" David's desire to show kindness to the descendants of the man who tried to kill him is a stunning picture of his godliness.

FOR JONATHAN'S SAKE: Jonathan and David had been intimate friends. Jonathan had helped David escape from Saul when the angry king was trying to kill him, and the two had sworn an oath that David would show kindness to Jonathan and his family when he came to be king (1 Samuel 20:14–15).

ZIBA AND MEPHIBOSHETH: *Saul's grandson Mephibosheth became lame at the time of Saul's death. He is now living far from David, and Saul's steward is running his estate.*

2. ZIBA: This man was evidently the chief steward of Saul's estate. After the deaths of Saul and Jonathan, the estate went to Mephibosheth, who became Ziba's employer.

3. THE KINDNESS OF GOD: It is significant that David considered his oath to Jonathan as a responsibility before God. He also saw it as a reflection of the kindness that God had so often shown to him. By keeping his oath and showing kindness to the house of Saul, David was imitating God.

LAME IN HIS FEET: Mephibosheth was a young boy when Saul and Jonathan died. When news of the deaths reached him, his nurse hastily grabbed him and fled for their lives. In the process, he fell and became lame in both his feet (2 Samuel 4:4). He was the son of Jonathan, grandson of Saul.

4. Lo Debar: Located about ten miles south of the Sea of Galilee. It may have been deliberate that he was situated a safe distance from the City of David.

Mercy and Grace: *David might have been expected to put Mephibosheth to death, but instead he grants him life—and much more.*

7. restore to you all the land: It was remarkable enough that King David would permit Mephibosheth to remain alive. As Saul's grandson, he was a potential threat to David's kingdom. But David went far beyond showing mercy—he showed him tremendous grace by restoring all the lands and possessions his family had lost when Saul died. It is possible that Saul's lands had been usurped by Ziba himself, as later events will make it clear that something was not quite right in Mephibosheth's household.

you shall eat bread at my table continually: David's actions toward Mephibosheth paint a picture of God's grace toward sinners. It would have been more than enough if God had merely offered forgiveness for sins—but He went far beyond that by adopting us as His children and inviting us to share freely of His blessings, even to join Him regularly at His table in the Lord's Supper, or communion service.

10. work the land for him: It is possible that David spelled out these details for Ziba because Ziba was appropriating Mephibosheth's property for his own gain.

fifteen sons and twenty servants: Again we are given details on Ziba that suggest he was a man of wealth and power. This wealth would cause problems for both him and Mephibosheth in the future. We will consider these characters in more detail in Study 9.

ᕹ First Impressions ᕹ

1. *What motivated David to honor Mephibosheth? If you had been in David's place, how would you have acted?*

2. *If you had been in Mephibosheth's place, how would you have reacted upon being called to the king's court? What would you have expected?*

3. *How would you have reacted if, like Mephibosheth, you were honored by dining with the king on a daily basis?*

4. *What was the difference between how the kings of pagan nations treated their potential rivals, and how David treated his?*

⌁ Some Key Principles ⌁

Fulfill your promises.

David and Jonathan loved one another like brothers, and either would willingly have laid down his life for the other. Jonathan, in fact, did risk his life by protecting David against Saul's murderous plans, risking the wrath of both father and king. The two men swore an oath of friendship, and David promised Jonathan that he would always show kindness to him and his family.

But Jonathan died young, fighting bravely against overwhelming odds with the Philistines. David, on the other hand, became king and had battles of his own to deal with. From the world's perspective, he would have been well within his kingly rights to put Mephibosheth to death, lest he prove a menace to his throne. It would have been more than gracious, in the world's eyes, for David to ignore Mephibosheth and let him live. But David took his oath very seriously; it was not enough merely to let Mephibosheth live—he went beyond that and deliberately showed compassion to Jonathan's son, simply because he had promised to do so.

David was imitating the character of God, who always keeps His promises. God's people, too, should take care to fulfill their word, whether given as a solemn oath (as in marriage vows) or merely a simple promise. To not do so invites divine judgment. In fact, according to James, it is better to not give your word at all than to give it and not keep it: "But above all, my brethren, do not swear, either by heaven or by earth or with any other oath," he wrote. Then, quoting Christ Himself (Matthew 5:37), he added, "But let your 'Yes' be 'Yes,' and your 'No,' 'No,' lest you fall into judgment" (James 5:12).

Do not take revenge.

David had served King Saul both loyally and exceptionally. As a young man, he had boldly faced the giant Goliath when all of Saul's army—and Saul himself—had been afraid to do so. He had later served at Saul's court, calming the king's strange moods with his songs.

Yet Saul had tried many times to murder David. He threw a spear at him in his own court, and he hunted him mercilessly for many years. David had demonstrated, even then, that he was loyal to Saul by not hurting him even when he had him completely at his mercy. Saul had wronged him significantly, and David had a considerable score to settle—yet he never took revenge into his own hands. Even when he was king and had the perfect right (in the world's eyes) to exact vengeance against Saul's heirs, he refrained—and went beyond, even to the point of showering gifts and honor upon Saul's grandson.

It can be very hard to resist taking revenge on people who have hurt us in the past. Our human nature sees it as simple justice to return evil for evil. But the Lord calls us to a higher standard, to act upon Christ's nature rather than our fallen human nature. In fact, Jesus commands us to go beyond withholding vengeance by returning good for evil, blessing those who curse us and doing good to those who harm us. "You have heard," said Jesus, "that it was said, 'You shall love your neighbor and hate your enemy.' But I say to you, love your enemies, bless those who curse you, do good to those who hate you, and pray for those who spitefully use you and persecute you, that you may be sons of your Father in heaven" (Matthew 5:43–45).

God shows us both mercy and grace.

Mercy is the act of withholding judgment upon a guilty person. A judge demonstrates mercy when he gives a criminal a second chance, or when he confers a judgment that is less than what the criminal deserves. Grace, however, goes beyond mercy, not merely withholding deserved judgment but also giving some undeserved gift.

Imagine if a criminal were found guilty of murder, and the judge determined for some reason to withhold the death penalty. That criminal would have received *mercy*, even if he still faced a stiff jail sentence. But now imagine if, further, that judge let the murderer go free from all judgment, and even gave him great wealth to start a new life. That criminal would have then received both mercy *and* grace—although at the expense of doing justice to the victims of the crime.

God's grace and mercy, however, are perfect. He did not ignore justice when He offered redemption to sinners—our sins brought the death penalty, and that penalty had to be paid. But God set us free from the penalty our sins deserved (mercy), made us heirs with His Son Jesus (grace), and paid for our sins (justice) Himself by giving His Son to die in our stead.

⤳ Digging Deeper ⤳

5. How does David's treatment of Mephibosheth demonstrate the character of God?

6. Why did David go to such lengths to fulfill his promise to Jonathan? What does this teach about the importance of keeping your word?

7. What is the difference between mercy and grace? How has God shown you mercy? How has He shown you grace?

8. When have you shown mercy or grace to someone else? Who is in need of your mercy at present?

ᴦ Taking It Personally ᴦ

9. *Do you generally keep your word? What promises have you forgotten to fulfill?*

10. *How do you treat people who mistreat you? What relationships might the Lord want you to improve in this regard?*

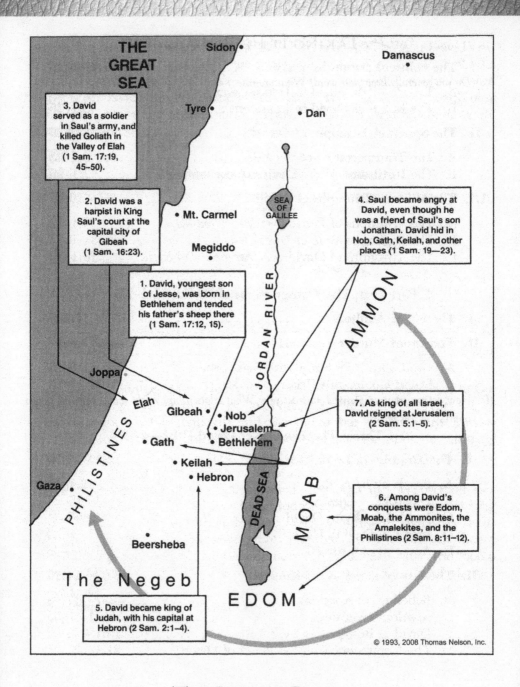

THE GREAT SEA

Sidon •

Damascus •

3. David served as a soldier in Saul's army, and killed Goliath in the Valley of Elah (1 Sam. 17:19, 45–50).

Tyre •

• Dan

2. David was a harpist in King Saul's court at the capital city of Gibeah (1 Sam. 16:23).

• Mt. Carmel

SEA OF GALILEE

4. Saul became angry at David, even though he was a friend of Saul's son Jonathan. David hid in Nob, Gath, Keilah, and other places (1 Sam. 19—23).

Megiddo •

1. David, youngest son of Jesse, was born in Bethlehem and tended his father's sheep there (1 Sam. 17:12, 15).

JORDAN RIVER

AMMON

Joppa •

Elah

Gibeah • • Nob

• Jerusalem

7. As king of all Israel, David reigned at Jerusalem (2 Sam. 5:1–5).

PHILISTINES

• Gath • Bethlehem

• Keilah

• Hebron

DEAD SEA

MOAB

Gaza •

6. Among David's conquests were Edom, Moab, the Ammonites, the Amalekites, and the Philistines (2 Sam. 8:11–12).

• Beersheba

The Negeb

5. David became king of Judah, with his capital at Hebron (2 Sam. 2:1–4).

E D O M

© 1993, 2008 Thomas Nelson, Inc.

THE LIFE OF DAVID

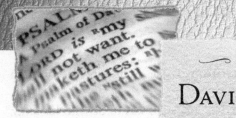

~ 4 ~
DAVID SINS

~ HISTORICAL BACKGROUND ~

The king of Ammon had died, and King David had sent ambassadors to express his condolences. But this gesture of peace and goodwill was greeted with contempt—the Ammonites disgraced the ambassadors and sent them home in shame. As a result, war broke out between the Ammonites and Israel, and Joab was leading the army in a siege on their city. David, however, was relaxing at home.

The king was responsible to lead his army in battle, and David's place during this conflict was on the battlefield, not on the roof of his house, taking a nap. We are not told why David chose to not be involved in the fighting, but in some measure he was shirking his responsibilities, and this temporary lack of diligence led him into very grievous sin.

Houses in David's day had flat roofs, and people would often conduct many mundane activities there. The cool breeze made it a good place for one's daily bathing, and the low wall surrounding the roof afforded an adequate screen from passersby in the street. Thus, a woman was not being immodest if she went on her roof to bathe—but unfortunately David's rooftop overlooked another—that of a very beautiful woman, and David was at home with nothing to do. In this sad chapter, we will see how one bad decision leads to another bad decision, and how one seemingly insignificant sin can have disastrous consequences.

~ READING 2 SAMUEL 11:1–27 ~

DAVID TAKES A HOLIDAY: *Israel is at war with the Ammonites, but David is indulging himself with some time off at home. The king's place, however, is with his army.*

I. IN THE SPRING OF THE YEAR: The events in this chapter are thought to have occurred roughly ten years after David established himself in Jerusalem.

THEY DESTROYED THE PEOPLE OF AMMON: These events are described in 2 Samuel 10.

BUT DAVID REMAINED AT JERUSALEM: The king's job was to be with his army, leading the war against the Ammonites. If David had been doing his job as he usually did, the following tragedy would not have occurred.

2. DAVID AROSE FROM HIS BED: This was in the late afternoon, not in the middle of the night. David had indulged himself with a nap, probably on the roof of his house, where he could enjoy the cool breeze. So far, David had done nothing overtly sinful; yet staying home while his army was at war and napping comfortably suggest he was indulging himself in unnecessary luxuries. Again, such behavior is not inherently wrong, yet it can place a person in the way of temptation—as we shall immediately see.

THE DEADLY TRIO: *David awakes from a nap and finds himself confronted with the lust of the eyes, the lust of the flesh, and the pride of life. The apostle John would later address this dangerous trio in 1 John 2:16: "For all that is in the world—the lust of the flesh, the lust of the eyes, and the pride of life—is not of the Father but is of the world."*

HE SAW A WOMAN BATHING: Roofs of buildings were level and were used frequently for a variety of activities, including bathing. David's rooftop was higher than the surrounding buildings, and his view of Bathsheba bathing was not due to any voyeurism; it was merely accidental.

THE WOMAN WAS VERY BEAUTIFUL TO BEHOLD: David's view of Bathsheba was inadvertent, as already noted, but here we can discern that he allowed his gaze to linger, rather than turning away his head as would have been proper. The first step in David's downward slide here was to shirk responsibility—motivated by the pride of his position. His second step was to indulge the lust of the eyes.

3. DAVID SENT AND INQUIRED ABOUT THE WOMAN: And here we have the third step in David's fall: he indulged the lust of the flesh.

URIAH THE HITTITE: Uriah was a very loyal soldier of David, and had earned renown for his deeds of valor. He was considered one of David's "mighty men" (2 Samuel 23:8, 39).

4. SENT . . . TOOK . . . LAY: This threefold sequence of sin is reminiscent of Eve in the garden of Eden. "So when the woman *saw* that the tree was good for food, that it was pleasant to the eyes, and a tree desirable to make one wise, she *took* of its fruit and *ate*" (Genesis 3:6, emphasis added). Like Eve, David gazed upon what was forbidden, and he permitted himself to be filled with desire. He then reached, took, and sinned. As a result, his life would never be the same.

SHE WAS CLEANSED FROM HER IMPURITY: This means that Bathsheba had completed her menstrual cycle and had followed the ceremonial cleansing prescribed by the law (Leviticus 15:19–30). This makes it clear that she was not pregnant by her husband, Uriah, when she had relations with David.

DAVID'S COVER-UP: *The king suddenly fears that people will learn of his sin, and he tries to cover it up. But he should have been more concerned with the Lord's opinion.*

5. I AM WITH CHILD: The Mosaic law prescribed the death penalty for those who committed adultery—both the man and the woman (Leviticus 20:10). David's role as king did not place him above God's law; on the contrary, as the leader of God's people, he was all the more accountable for this sin.

6. SEND ME URIAH THE HITTITE: David began this process by shirking his responsibility as commander of Israel's army. Here he openly abused that position of power by arbitrarily calling one of his best fighters home from battle merely to cover his own transgression.

7. DAVID ASKED HOW JOAB WAS DOING: This ridiculous questioning must have seemed peculiar to Uriah. The king could have gained such basic information from any underling, and hardly required the perspective of one of his best warriors. Yet there is no record that Uriah questioned his king's intentions; he was a good soldier, and everything we are told indicates that he was a man of strong character.

8. GO DOWN TO YOUR HOUSE AND WASH YOUR FEET: In other words, David was urging Uriah to go home and relax. He even sent along a gift of food, intending that the couple enjoy a romantic dinner together. He was obviously hoping that Uriah would take advantage of the furlough to be intimate with his wife.

9. URIAH SLEPT AT THE DOOR OF THE KING'S HOUSE: It is a natural reflex to attempt to hide one's sin, to prevent others from discovering things that we are ashamed of. But this is not what God calls His people to do; rather, we are to confess our sins and not hide them. David's cover-up failed, as it was God's will to bring his sin to light. As Moses warned the people of Israel, "be sure your sin will find you out" (Numbers 32:23).

11. DWELLING IN TENTS: Uriah felt that it would be wrong for him to enjoy luxury while God and His people were living in tents. This is just one of the ways in which Uriah unintentionally demonstrated that at this point he was a man of nobler character than David.

SHALL I THEN GO TO MY HOUSE: Uriah had a strong sense of his responsibility here. How could he indulge himself in the comforts of home while his fellow soldiers were fighting in battle? He understood that his place was with the army, providing a strong contrast to David's present self-indulgence.

13. HE MADE HIM DRUNK: David did not give up. He thought that Uriah might loosen his standards if only he had alcohol in him. Notice how David's sin and cover-up caused him to lead others into sin.

> **DAVID COMMITS MURDER:** *The cover-up has failed, thanks to Uriah's loyal character, so David resorts to the next expedient. He orders Uriah's death.*

14. SENT IT BY THE HAND OF URIAH: This reveals the ugliness of sin. David had committed adultery with the wife of one of his most loyal followers, and had further used Uriah's loyalty in an attempt to cover his own sin. Finally, he abused Uriah's trust by having him deliver the order commanding his own murder.

15. THAT HE MAY BE STRUCK DOWN AND DIE: David thought that, if Uriah was dead, people would assume that Bathsheba was carrying Uriah's child. This plan worked for a time. It is important to note that David's sin of lust led to the sin of adultery, which led to the sin of cover-up and abuse of power, which finally led to the sin of murder. Sin breeds more sin, and the only way to stop the destructive cycle is to repent and confess our sins.

17. THE SERVANTS OF DAVID FELL: As Joab revealed in his message to the king (v. 21), this sortie was probably motivated by David's order for Uriah's death. Joab probably would not have sent his men against the fortified city at this point, knowing that he would suffer large casualties. Here again we see that many innocent lives were affected by David's sin.

21. A WOMAN WHO CAST A PIECE OF A MILLSTONE: See Judges 9:52–53.

URIAH THE HITTITE IS DEAD ALSO: Joab was absolving himself of any responsibility for Uriah's death—and also for the poor military leadership. He was subtly reminding David that he was merely following the king's orders. It is also a tragic commentary that he referred to Uriah as "your servant Uriah." David had betrayed one of his most loyal soldiers.

> **GOD IS NOT MOCKED:** *David's attempt at cover-up seems to have worked finally, and he hardens his heart to his own guilt. But God is not finished with the issue.*

25. DO NOT LET THIS THING DISPLEASE YOU: The final step in David's cycle of sins was that he became hardened to his own guilt—and he urged others to join in hardening their hearts as well. When we indulge our sinful desires, we gradually harden our hearts to the Lord's convictions, searing our consciences to the point that we no longer feel any guilt over sin.

26. SHE MOURNED FOR HER HUSBAND: It is interesting that there is no mention of David mourning. He had not yet repented of his sins.

27. THE THING THAT DAVID HAD DONE DISPLEASED THE LORD: This is an ominous ending to this passage. David had successfully covered up his sins, hiding them from the eyes of men—but it is impossible to cover our sin from the eyes of God. The effects of David's wrongdoing would be far-reaching and profound, as we will see in future studies.

⌁ FIRST IMPRESSIONS ⌁

1. What led David to be tempted by sin? What might he have done to avoid the temptation?

2. How did David's sin multiply in this chapter? List all of the different sins David committed here.

3. Describe all that David did to cover up his sin. Why did his first plans fail?

4. How does Uriah contrast with David in this passage? How are the two men different? How are they similar?

∼ Some Key Principles ∼

The Lord calls us to confess our sins, not to cover them up.

David slipped into a downward spiral of sin, beginning with self-indulgence and leading to adultery with Bathsheba. His immediate concern seemed to be that people would find out what he had done—but he should have been more concerned with how it would affect his relationship with God. This misdirected fear led him to attempt a cover-up, as if the worst thing that could come as a result of his sin was that someone might find out. It did not occur to him that the Lord saw, and the Lord was displeased.

In our next study, we will see that David eventually did confess his sin and repent before the Lord, and the Lord forgave him and restored him to fellowship. But it would have been far better if he had repented immediately—better still if he had not committed the sin in the first place. His attempts to cover his transgressions led to more sin, and caused increased suffering for others around him.

God wants His people to refrain from sinful behavior, but He also knows that we are sinners by birth. Being born again into the family of Christ does not mean that we will never sin again. "If we say that we have no sin, we deceive ourselves, and the truth is not in us," wrote John the apostle (1 John 1:8). We will sin. But when we do, the Lord calls us to confess and repent immediately, not to try and conceal it. "If we confess our sins, He is faithful and just to forgive us our sins and to cleanse us from all unrighteousness" (v. 9). Confession leads to forgiveness and reconciliation, but cover-up leads to further sin and suffering.

Sin breeds more sin.

David began his problems in this chapter when he indulged his flesh, avoiding the responsibilities of leading his army in battle. This led to a temptation that he would have avoided otherwise. He sinned openly when he gazed upon Bathsheba during her bath, which inflamed his lust. This lust led to the sin of sexual immorality with a woman who was not his wife, which led him to err further by trying to hide his guilt from the people around him. And this sin led to the sin of murder.

It is important to understand that David alone was responsible for this tragic sequence of sin. The book of James bears this out: "Let no one say when he is tempted, 'I am tempted by God'; for God cannot be tempted by evil, nor does He Himself tempt anyone. But each one is tempted when he is drawn away by *his own* desires and enticed. Then, when desire has conceived, it gives birth to sin; and sin, when it is full-grown, brings forth death" (1:13–15, emphasis added). *Death.* Did you catch that? David made one bad decision, which led to another bad decision, and another—and the end result was the death of many innocent men.

Like David, we can find ourselves in a downward spiral of sin when we indulge our fleshly desires. The good news, however, is that God offers grace to cover our sin and the Holy Spirit to convict us of sin—and to help us avoid it in the first place.

Faithfulness to our responsibilities can protect us from disaster.

David's tragic failure in this chapter could have been avoided altogether if he had remained faithful in his responsibilities. The role of the king was to lead the army in battle, and his place was on the battlefield along with Joab—not receiving reports of the distant conflict while he sat comfortably at home. Uriah, on the other hand, presents a startling contrast in this regard. He never lost sight of his responsibilities as a soldier and a servant of the king, and this faithfulness inadvertently foiled David's intended cover-up.

Joseph's life (Genesis 37–41) gives us an example of how faithfulness can not only protect a person but can bring with it great blessings. Joseph was a mere slave in the house of Potiphar, yet he was faithful to his master and diligent in his duties. This faithfulness led to being falsely accused of adultery with his master's wife, and he found himself in prison for a crime he didn't commit. Yet even there he remained faithful to the small tasks the Lord gave him, and his faithfulness ultimately led him to a position of authority over all Egypt.

At times, our responsibilities can seem small and insignificant, and it is easy to justify shirking them, as David did. But when we avoid our responsibilities, we are often setting ourselves up for sin. When we are faithful to our responsibilities, our faithfulness often is blessed by the Lord.

↳ DIGGING DEEPER ↲

5.   *Why did David try to cover his sin? What motivated the cover-up?*

6.   Who suffered from David's sin? Who was responsible for their suffering?

7.   Why is there no reference to God or God's view of David's actions until the final verse of the chapter? What does that teach us about David's thinking? Why do you think David never sought the Lord in this chapter?

8. Put the following sins into your own words, and give examples for each.

Lust of the flesh:

Lust of the eyes:

Pride of life:

⌁ TAKING IT PERSONALLY ⌁

9. How faithful are you to the responsibilities God has given you? In what areas do you need to be more diligent?

10. Is there any sin in your life that you are trying to cover up? Take time right now to confess it before the Lord.

~5~
DAVID REPENTS

⤳ HISTORICAL BACKGROUND ⤶

As this study opens, time has passed since David's sins of adultery and murder. He has married Bathsheba, and she has borne him a son. Yet even now, David has not repented of his sins and apparently feels that he has successfully covered them up. The people in his court, as far as we know, have said nothing of the matter—whether or not they are aware of what David has done.

But God *is* aware, and He is not content to pretend that nothing wrong has been done. David thought he could cover his sin because he was viewing it from the perspective of the world—as long as nobody gets upset, there's no problem. God's perspective, however, is vastly different: David's sin has damaged his relationship with the Lord, and He will not permit that to go unresolved.

In this chapter, we will meet the prophet Nathan once again, but this time his conversation with David is not as pleasant as it was in Study 2. This time, God has sent Nathan to confront the king with his grievous sins, and to lead him to confess and repent before the Lord. Nathan's approach to the confrontation is interesting: he does not initially "get in David's face" and challenge him with his deeds. Instead, he tells David a story about two neighbors—and that story will lead David to see his sins from God's point of view, rather than the world's.

⤳ READING 2 SAMUEL 12:1–25 ⤶

NATHAN CONFRONTS DAVID: *David has married Bathsheba, they have a new child, and it seems that he has gotten away with murder. But then God has His say in the matter.*

1. THEN: It had probably been about a year since David's adultery with Bathsheba. He had murdered her husband, Uriah, and married Bathsheba prior to the child's birth, and we can assume that the child was at least a few months old at this time.

THE LORD SENT NATHAN TO DAVID: David had sent Uriah to Joab with a message commanding murder, and Joab had sent a messenger back to David, announcing that the murder had been accomplished. But the Lord had a message of His own for David, and it would not bring him the relief that Joab's message had.

HE CAME TO HIM: Nathan confronted David not with a direct challenge but with a parable. This approach enabled David to see his sin from God's perspective, forcing him to stop looking at it from man's point of view.

TWO MEN: It is interesting to note the differences between the two men, representing David and Uriah. One was very rich, the other very poor, suggesting that Uriah was not a man of means. One man had many flocks and herds, the other only one cherished lamb. David had many wives and concubines, while Uriah was faithfully married only to Bathsheba. The rich man in the parable also used his herds and flocks for food and income, while the poor man kept his lamb as a pet—suggesting the deep, devoted love that Uriah had for his wife, contrasted with David's self-serving attitude that led to his using Bathsheba merely to gratify his fleshly desires.

3. LAY IN HIS BOSOM: This is a poignant depiction of Uriah's evident love for Bathsheba. If Nathan's parable represented an accurate picture of Uriah's household, then David's sin destroyed a very godly family.

4. A TRAVELER CAME TO THE RICH MAN: This is an illuminating metaphor of temptation, the lusts and desires of man's heart, which come and go without our bidding. David had arisen from a casual nap, not intending to look around for another man's wife—yet the temptation had come upon him suddenly and unexpectedly.

REFUSED TO TAKE FROM HIS OWN FLOCK: David could easily have found comfort with one of his many wives, but that is not the nature of lust. Lust demands that which is forbidden or unattainable, making what is good and proper seem detestable. The rich man in the proverb was wicked because he refused to sacrifice one of his many lambs, insisting on taking the poor man's cherished pet instead. This is exactly what David had done.

PREPARED IT FOR THE MAN WHO HAD COME TO HIM: Nathan was forcing David to recognize that he had sacrificed Bathsheba, Uriah, and others on the altar of his own lust. He had taken Bathsheba to satisfy his fleshly craving, just as the rich man in the parable had sacrificed the poor man's lamb to satisfy the traveling salesman.

THE KING PASSES JUDGMENT: *David is outraged by Nathan's story, and passes a harsh sentence on the rich man—thereby condemning himself to death.*

5. DAVID'S ANGER WAS GREATLY AROUSED: David had taken Nathan's story literally, thinking that someone in his kingdom had committed this grievous sin. The truth is, of course, that someone had—but that someone was the king himself. David's anger also demonstrated that he had finally seen his own sin from God's perspective, and his righteous indignation was stirred up. But he could not become indignant against his own sin until he saw it from God's viewpoint.

SHALL SURELY DIE: It is interesting that the law did not require the death penalty for stealing an ox or lamb, but merely restitution. When we harbor unrepentant sin, we tend to judge others more harshly, perhaps because it makes us feel less guilty about our own sins if we increase the guilt of others' sins. Yet in passing this harsh verdict, David was unwittingly condemning himself to death—which *was* the correct judgment for both murder and adultery.

6. HE SHALL RESTORE FOURFOLD FOR THE LAMB: This actually was the correct judgment for the crime of stealing a lamb, according to the law (Exodus 22:1). There is also a certain dark, ironic humor in condemning a man to death *and* to restitution. But David's judgment, which he pronounced in a cavalier fashion upon a hypothetical stranger, would come upon his own head in the future. Four of his own sons would die tragically: Bathsheba's first son, Amnon, Absalom, and Adonijah.

BECAUSE HE HAD NO PITY: David's own words condemned another element of his sin: he'd shown no pity on his faithful warrior Uriah. Even after committing the sin of adultery, he might still have been moved by remorse for destroying another man's marriage—and certainly pity toward such a good soldier as Uriah. David's sin was actually far greater than that of the rich man in the parable, for the rich man merely stole the poor man's lamb—he didn't also murder the man himself.

THE LORD SPEAKS: *Nathan now confronts David openly with his sin, and pronounces the Lord's judgment—which is far less harsh than David's rash judgment.*

8. I ALSO WOULD HAVE GIVEN YOU MUCH MORE: The Lord had blessed David beyond all measure, promising to establish his throne forever and to bring the Redeemer of mankind through his lineage—yet He would willingly have given him even more if David had only asked. God wants His children to ask Him to meet their needs, rather than reaching out for themselves and taking what does not belong to them.

9. DESPISED THE COMMANDMENT OF THE LORD: When we disobey God's commands, we demonstrate contempt for His Word—and ultimately contempt for the person of Jesus Christ, the Incarnate Word. Thus, in verse 10, the Lord told David, "You have despised Me."

10. THE SWORD SHALL NEVER DEPART FROM YOUR HOUSE: The remainder of David's days as king were marked by tragedy and betrayal, most of it coming from his own household. As David betrayed the sanctity of Uriah's marriage, so David's son would betray his father's marriage bed. As David had brought the sword on an innocent man, so David's sons would bring the sword upon one another.

11. HE SHALL LIE WITH YOUR WIVES IN THE SIGHT OF THIS SUN: David's son Absalom would later lie publicly with his father's concubines (2 Samuel 16).

12. YOU DID IT SECRETLY: God promises that those things we do in secret will be brought into the light of day for all to see. Jesus said, "For there is nothing hidden which will not be revealed, nor has anything been kept secret but that it should come to light" (Mark 4:22).

DAVID REPENTS: *Here we see one reason why David was called "a man after God's own heart." When confronted with his sin, he confesses immediately.*

---

13. I HAVE SINNED AGAINST THE LORD: Here David reveals what it means to be a man after God's own heart. He had sinned greatly, yet when confronted, he did not equivocate. He did not try to justify his actions or blame his sin on someone else; instead, he confessed openly that he was guilty as charged. Notice also that David knew he had sinned against the Lord, not merely against Bathsheba, Uriah, and his soldiers.

THE LORD ALSO HAS PUT AWAY YOUR SIN: This is the glorious message of the gospel, that God forgives even the most wicked sinner if he will confess and repent.

YOU SHALL NOT DIE: The law demanded that murderers and adulterers be put to death, and David was guilty of both crimes. Yet God, in His grace and mercy, forgave David and set him free from that penalty, just as the sacrifice of Christ sets free those who accept His gift of salvation. The Bible says that "all have sinned and fall short of the glory of God" (Romans 3:23) and are therefore subject to death. God's justice must be satisfied, so someone had to pay the penalty for sin. Christ Himself paid that penalty for all who would receive Him, satisfying God's justice while also offering grace to the guilty.

14. HOWEVER: The Lord's mercy on David applied to his eternal relationship with God, but it did not exempt him from suffering the temporal consequences of his sin. God's forgiveness of sin does not always remove the consequences of sin in our lifetime, as David would experience for the rest of his days.

YOU HAVE GIVEN GREAT OCCASION TO THE ENEMIES OF THE LORD: David's sin had displayed a contempt for God's Word, and for the Lord Himself; similarly, his sin would encourage the enemies of God to demonstrate a similar contempt for the things of the Lord. Sin affects more than those involved in it. As we have seen already, one man's sin caused suffering and death to people who were completely innocent, and it would also provide occasion for others to blaspheme the name of the Lord.

THE CHILD . . . SHALL SURELY DIE: Yet one more innocent life would be forfeited due to David's sin.

JUDGMENT AND GRACE: *The little child dies as God foretold, but God's grace follows His judgment. David and Bathsheba have another son, Solomon, who would become king.*

---

18. THE SERVANTS OF DAVID WERE AFRAID TO TELL HIM: The servants misunderstood David's weeping and fasting over the sick child. They assumed he was grieving, when in fact he was interceding for the child's life. When the child finally died, David knew that the Lord's answer to his prayers had been no—and he had no further occasion to make that intercession.

20. HE WENT INTO THE HOUSE OF THE LORD AND WORSHIPED: Some might have become angry with God for taking the life of the child, but David recognized that God had been both just and merciful. His response, even in the midst of great sorrow, was to worship God, and in this he again demonstrated what it means to be a man after God's own heart.

23. I SHALL GO TO HIM: David demonstrated great faith in God's promises, believing by faith that he would one day meet his son again in eternity. It is clear that David fully expected to see his baby again after his own death. This is one of the many examples in Scripture showing how the Lord extends His saving grace to infants who are too young to understand evil and to reject God. [1]

25. JEDIDIAH: Nathan called Solomon Jedidiah, which meant "beloved of the Lord." This is another demonstration of God's immense grace, bringing great blessing even out of gross sin.

---

1. This is not to suggest that infants are somehow born morally good or even morally neutral. Of course, all people are born into sin, as David himself wrote (Psalm 51:5; 58:3). Nevertheless, Scripture often teaches that the Lord, because of His mercy, does not condemn to hell infants too young to understand what they are doing (Ecclesiastes 6:3–6; Job 3:16–19; 1 Kings 14:13; Matthew 18:3). For more on this topic, see my book *Safe in the Arms of God* (Thomas Nelson, 2003).

⌒ First Impressions ⌒

1. Why did Nathan have to confront David about his sin? What prevented David from repenting sooner?

2. How did Nathan's parable expose the true nature of David's sins? What elements in the parable related directly to those sins?

3. Why did God say that David had despised Him? In what ways do we despise God when we sin?

4. Why did David go to the temple and worship God after his child died? What does this reveal about David's character?

ᗧ SOME KEY PRINCIPLES ᗧ

God's people must view sin from God's perspective.

When David committed adultery, he viewed his actions from man's perspective. His major concern was to prevent other people from knowing what he had done, and this led him to attempt a cover-up. As we have seen already, however, his cover-up led to more sin and further attempts to conceal it.

If David had viewed his sin of adultery from God's point of view, on the other hand, he would have been quick to confess and repent. Man is concerned with what other people will think, but God is interested in how our sin damages our relationship with Him. David was worried about his reputation as king, while God was thinking of his eternal fellowship.

51

Today, the world tells us that the most important priority is appearances, placing great value on outward show while claiming that there are no eternal consequences for our actions. God, however, is focused on eternity, so He wants His people to see every sin as something that puts distance between them and Him.

Sin brings temporal consequences that sometimes cannot be avoided.

When David confessed his sin and repented, the Lord showed him mercy and grace. The law demanded that he should be put to death for both adultery and murder, but God commuted that sentence—and went even further by blessing him with Solomon. Nevertheless, the temporal results of his sins were not removed: David's family would suffer greatly for his transgressions, as would the entire nation of Israel when Absalom attempted to overthrow his father's throne.

God shows His infinite mercy to sinners who repent, providing us forgiveness and eternal life—and much, much more. Yet there are times when our sinful behaviors will produce bad fruit that does not go away. We may retain scars or weaknesses that affect our lives and the lives of those we love, results of former sins, which remain with us for years or even a lifetime. This principle applies to Christians and non-Christians alike.

Sin can seem alluring during times of temptation, but the end result is always the same: death. As we learn to see sin from God's perspective, we will also see that it never pays—it is always best to live according to God's Word, avoiding the deadly scars and consequences that would result otherwise.

The man after God's own heart is quick to repent.

One can hardly say that David repented quickly after his sin of adultery, since it was probably a year or so later when Nathan confronted him. If he had confessed his adultery immediately, he would have avoided adding the sin of murder to his guilt. If he had repented immediately of his lust when gazing at Bathsheba, he would have avoided the adultery altogether.

Nevertheless, David did repent and confess immediately when he was brought face-to-face with his sin as God viewed it, and in doing so he demonstrated that he was a man after God's own heart. He recognized that he had sinned against the Lord, not merely against his fellow man, and he understood that his sin had separated him from God's fellowship.

The goal for God's people should be to avoid sin altogether, but when we do sin, we should be quick to confess and repent. We cannot hope to hide our sins from God, so cover-ups are of no avail. When we delay confession, we only deprive ourselves of full fellowship with the Father, and cheat ourselves out of His blessings.

⤳ DIGGING DEEPER ⤳

5. *Why did Nathan use a parable to confront David? Why not a direct accusation? What does this teach about the nature of confession?*

6. *Why did David condemn to death the rich man in Nathan's parable? What did this reveal about David's attitude toward his own guilt?*

7. *Why did God not condemn David to die, even though the law demanded the death penalty for both murder and adultery? What does this reveal about God's character?*

53

8. Why did God not remove the judgment against David's family? What does this reveal about the nature of sin? about God's character?

↵ TAKING IT PERSONALLY ↵

9. Are there any sins in your life of which you have not repented? What is preventing you from confessing them to the Lord right now?

10. How does a person gain God's perspective concerning sin and holiness? What are you doing at present to gain that perspective?

Section 2:

Characters

IN THIS SECTION:

~6~
AMNON AND TAMAR

2 SAMUEL 13

~ CHARACTERS' BACKGROUND ~

In the previous study, we learned that, after David's sin, the prophet Nathan confronted the king and brought a prophecy from the Lord that the sword would never depart from his household. It did not take long for that prophecy to begin to unfold, and the events that followed were tragic and heartbreaking.

David's household was ripe for such conflict, as he had numerous wives and concubines who had borne him many sons. That situation begged for jealousies and strife, especially as David's sons began vying for their father's throne. David's firstborn son was Amnon, whose mother was Ahinoam. By rights, Amnon was the natural successor to David's throne—but Absalom had other ideas. Absalom was born to Maacah, herself the daughter of a king, and he evidently felt himself better qualified to take his father's place. (We will take a closer look at Absalom in Study 7.)

But another problem also arose within David's mixed family: his eldest son developed an unhealthy desire for his half sister, Tamar. This dangerous situation was made all the more volatile because Amnon, the heir apparent, was lusting after the *full* sister of his rival Absalom. When Amnon raped Tamar, he gave Absalom an excuse to murder him—and the seeds of revolution were sown.

~ READING 2 SAMUEL 13:1–39 ~

LOVESICK: *David has many wives and many children—a recipe for disaster. One of his sons begins to lust after his half sister.*

1. AFTER THIS: That is, sometime after David was confronted by Nathan concerning his adultery and murder. The author was letting us know that there was a connection between David's sin and what occurred in this chapter. The fulfillment of the Lord's prophecy (2 Samuel 12:10) was beginning to unfold.

Absalom: David's third son, born to him through Maacah, his fourth wife. David had many wives, and it will be important to understand the interrelationship between his children in this chapter, as rivalries and resentments become apparent.

Tamar: Meaning "palm tree." Her mother was also Maacah, making her the full sister of Absalom.

Amnon: Amnon was David's son, by Ahinoam, David's second wife. Thus Amnon was a half brother to both Tamar and Absalom. He was also David's firstborn, which might have added some tension in his relationship with Absalom, the third-born son. By birthright, Amnon was the heir to David's throne, while Absalom would receive little by way of inheritance.

loved her: Amnon's love turned out to be merely lust, as this chapter will reveal.

2. he became sick: The picture of the lovesick young man—pining away in unrequited longing for the woman of his dreams—is popular in modern art. But this chapter will demonstrate that such sentiments may only be a thin disguise for lust. Amnon was obsessed with his desire for his half sister to the point that he could think of nothing else; he could not even undertake his normal daily duties.

she was a virgin: A woman's virginity was protected and cherished at all costs in David's time. Unmarried daughters were kept apart from men, not permitted to be in a man's company without family members present. Amnon, however, would have been in contact with her because of their family relationship.

it was improper for Amnon to do anything to her: It would have been inappropriate for a young man to have any intimacy with a woman to whom he was not married, but the impropriety in this instance was more than that, since the law forbade a man to marry his sister—even a half sister (Leviticus 18:11).

A Crafty Counselor: *David's nephew Jonadab is a cunning man, and he shares the subtle craftiness of the devil. His advice leads to disaster for David's household.*

3. Jonadab: This was David's brother's son, making him Amnon's cousin.

a very crafty man: Craftiness, or cunning, is not considered a virtue in Scripture. The serpent in Eden "was more cunning than any beast of the field which the Lord God had made" (Genesis 3:1), and his lies deceived Eve into eating the forbidden fruit. In a similar manner, the cunning of Jonadab would lead Amnon into acting on his lusts.

4. the king's son: On one hand, Jonadab was merely pointing out the obvious, that the son of the king should have everything he needed to keep him content. But on a more subtle level, he was flattering Amnon by suggesting that, as the heir apparent to his father's throne, he had a right to reach out and take whatever he desired. Compare Satan's temptation of Eve in Genesis 3.

5. PRETEND TO BE ILL: Jonadab's counsel was wicked from the outset, as he suggested that Amnon deceive his father. A crafty person is deceitful and manipulative, using the very tools the devil used to deceive Eve.

6. THAT I MAY EAT FROM HER HAND: This was very childish behavior, to suggest that a grown man could not eat any food unless it was prepared in his sight by a specific person. The fact that David acquiesced suggests that the king was excessively indulgent with his sons—as we will see more fully in David's dealings with Absalom.

10. BRING THE FOOD INTO THE BEDROOM: Amnon's sin was even more despicable when we see how he betrayed his sister's trust. Tamar unhesitatingly complied with his request because his wicked intentions never entered her mind. She was the one character in this tragic tale who showed no guile—and it was she who suffered the most.

TAMAR PLEADS FOR RIGHTEOUSNESS: *Tamar demonstrates that she has a heart for God, wanting to do what is right. But her brother refuses to listen.*

12. NO SUCH THING SHOULD BE DONE IN ISRAEL: Tamar made every attempt to escape the clutches of lustful Amnon, giving him three clear reasons why he should not force himself upon her. The first reason is the most significant: such an act was forbidden by God's law, and as such it should not be committed by any of God's people.

13. WHERE COULD I TAKE MY SHAME?: Tamar's second argument against Amnon's behavior was to point out that he would bring shame upon her if he continued. Even though she was fighting for her innocence, she would probably be unable to find a man who wanted to marry her once she had lost her virginity. She would be disgraced in David's court.

YOU WOULD BE LIKE ONE OF THE FOOLS IN ISRAEL: Tamar's third argument was to point out that Amnon would also bring disgrace upon himself if he continued. The people would recognize that he cared more about his own passions than about obeying God's commands. This might also jeopardize his claims to his father's throne in the future. Tamar was trying to make her brother see that he was sinning against God, against her, and against himself.

HE WILL NOT WITHHOLD ME FROM YOU: As already stated, such a marriage was forbidden by God's law, so it was unlikely that David would actually have sanctioned it. Yet Tamar was in a desperate situation, and was urging her brother to restrain his passions.

15. AMNON HATED HER EXCEEDINGLY: This is generally the sad result of indulged lusts. Once the desire is sated, the former attraction turns to revulsion. Amnon's hatred was probably based upon a degree of self-loathing as he saw the immense wickedness he had committed, and this would be yet another bad way of dealing with his passions. Rather than hating his sister, whom he had wronged, he should have hated his own sin and sought forgiveness from God and from his family. In this, we find a strong contrast to David's response when he was confronted with his sin: David repented, but Amnon blamed others.

16. THIS EVIL OF SENDING ME AWAY: Tamar feared that it would appear to others as though she had willingly cooperated with her brother's sin—or even that she had initiated it.

17. BOLT THE DOOR BEHIND HER: Amnon disgraced his sister yet further when he called in a servant and had her thrown out, thus effectively telling the household that she had seduced him. Bolting the door behind her gave the appearance that Amnon feared she might try to come back and lead him into more sin.

ABSALOM GETS REVENGE: *David fails to address the sin of his son, so another son plots evil. Absalom eventually murders his half brother.*

19. TAMAR PUT ASHES ON HER HEAD: Tamar's response to this sin contrasts dramatically with that of Amnon. The ashes on her head, the torn robe, and the loud lamenting were a public declaration of grief, shame, and loss. Amnon hoped to hide his sin, as David had done, while Tamar realized that sin cannot remain hidden.

20. DO NOT TAKE THIS THING TO HEART: Absalom's counsel is as bad as that of Jonadab. He was telling his sister to pretend that sin is nothing to worry about, and his counsel is still given by the world today. In reality, however, Absalom had his own plans for revenge, and probably also saw this event as an excuse to remove his brother Amnon from the succession to the throne.

21. HE WAS VERY ANGRY: David's wrath was justified, and he should have addressed the sin with quick action. But there is no record that he did anything about it, and it is quite possible that he felt it would have been hypocritical of him to punish Amnon after he had committed similar sins himself. Whatever his motivation, David did not fulfill his obligations both as king and as Tamar's father, and his excessive leniency would later breed more trouble in the household.

28. ABSALOM HAD COMMANDED HIS SERVANTS: It is interesting that both Absalom and Amnon used their servants to do their dirty work (v. 17). In this, they were mimicking their father, who had Joab arrange the murder of Uriah in battle.

KILL HIM: David's two eldest sons committed sexual immorality and murder, just as their father had done. Absalom may also have been motivated by hopes of securing the throne for himself, as Amnon's death made him the heir apparent. (There is no mention of David's second son Chileab [2 Samuel 3:3], which suggests that he was no longer alive at this point.) The law did prescribe the death penalty for Amnon's crime (Leviticus 18), but it was not Absalom's place to execute that judgment.

33. LET NOT MY LORD THE KING TAKE THE THING TO HIS HEART: Here we find Jonadab offering the same wicked counsel to David as Absalom had given earlier. The wisdom of the world tells us to gloss over sin, but God's Word teaches clearly that sin brings consequences.

37. ABSALOM FLED: David's household was falling apart, just as God had predicted.
KING OF GESHUR: This was Absalom's grandfather, his mother's father.

⤳ First Impressions ⤳

1. Why was Amnon so consumed with desire for Tamar? What was the nature of his "love" for her?

2. What reasons did Tamar give to her brother for avoiding sin? How do these concepts apply to sin in general?

3. Why did Amnon come to despise Tamar? What does this reveal about his desires? about sin in general?

4. What was ungodly in Jonadab's counsel to Amnon? to David? Why did each man accept his counsel, rather than reject it?

⌁ Some Key Principles ⌁

God's people must restrain their fleshly desires.

David arose from a nap and inadvertently saw a woman bathing. If he had turned away, he would not have become consumed with desire for her. Instead, he permitted his desires to have their way—and committed adultery. His son later followed his example by not reining in his lust for Tamar, and that lust bore horrible fruit.

Temptation comes to all people. As long as we live in fleshly bodies, we will experience physical desires. The desire itself is not sin; the sin comes when we yield to desires that are contrary to God's Word. It is not a sin to become hungry, but it can be a sin when we yield to the temptation of gluttony.

God wants His children to be characterized by self-control. The world teaches that we should gratify our every desire, claiming that it is not healthy to restrain natural impulses. But God's Word warns us that the cravings of the flesh lead to death, while righteousness evidenced by self-control leads to life.

"As righteousness leads to life, so he who pursues evil pursues it to his own death" (Proverbs 11:19).

Revenge belongs to God.

Amnon's sin was grievous, and it needed to be addressed. This was David's job as king, and he should not have ignored it even though it was committed by his own son. Nevertheless, this did not justify Absalom's taking the matter into his own hands. When Absalom killed Amnon, he did not enact justice; he carried out revenge. By doing so, he was merely committing another gross sin before God, not carrying out God's design.

It is a natural human response to want justice, and this in itself is not wrong. Yet God's people do well to remember that we do not receive what we deserve from God—we receive grace, not condemnation. When someone harms us in some way, our flesh wants to get even, demanding that justice be served. But this is another facet of restraining our fleshly desires, choosing instead to forgive and leave the matter in God's hands.

The person after God's own heart will even go beyond refraining from taking revenge by actually doing good to those who have harmed him. Jesus said, "Love your enemies, bless those who curse you, do good to those who hate you, and pray for those who spitefully use you and persecute you, that you may be sons of your Father in heaven" (Matthew 5:44–45). This is exactly what Christ did for us, pouring out blessings on us when all we deserved was death.

Beware of ungodly counsel.

Jonadab saw that Amnon was pining away after a woman, so he offered advice on how to gratify his carnal cravings. And, like most false counselors, he seemed to be well versed in the intrigues of everyone around him, appearing at the most opportune times to give his advice, as he did when David was grieving.

He began his counsel to Amnon by suggesting that the young man deceive his father. Amnon should have recognized that Jonadab's advice was ungodly and rejected it outright. Instead, he followed Jonadab's poisonous "wisdom," though he was not compelled to do so.

Today, the world bombards us with ungodly counsel that, like Jonadab's, often sounds wise and expedient, but God's people are called to weigh every teaching against the teachings of Scripture. Godly counsel never advises us to disobey God's commands. Had Amnon considered that, he may actually have succeeded his father on the throne.

∽ DIGGING DEEPER ∽

5. *What should Amnon have done about his desires for Tamar? What would have been a godly way of dealing with the situation?*

6. *How did the actions of Amnon and Absalom mirror David's life? How did they differ?*

7. Why did David not address the sin of Amnon? of Absalom? How might things have ended if he had punished Amnon in the first place?

8. What role did Jonadab play in these two tragedies? How much responsibility did he bear for the sins? How much responsibility did Amnon and Absalom bear?

9. When have you received ungodly counsel? How can you tell when someone is giving you godly advice?

10. Is there an area of fleshly desire that is controlling your life at present? What must you do to restrain those desires?

~ 7 ~
ABSALOM

2 SAMUEL 15, 18

⌁ CHARACTER'S BACKGROUND ⌁

After murdering his brother Amnon, Absalom fled Jerusalem and went to live with his grandfather, the king of Geshur. He lived there for three years, while David mourned for him and yearned to see him again. Joab eventually intervened (using a tactic that was very similar to Nathan's confrontation in Study 5), and persuaded David to send word to Absalom, permitting him to return to Jerusalem.

Once Absalom returned, however, David refused to see him, perhaps because he was torn between fatherly love and guilt over the fact that he had not executed justice after the murder of Amnon. Whatever his motives, Absalom was forced to content himself living in Jerusalem without access to his father. In this, however, he was anything but content.

So Absalom took matters into his own hands. He had his servants set fire to Joab's crops, forcing a confrontation with Joab, the leader of David's army. Joab then went to David and interceded, and David relented and restored his son to a full loving relationship. One might expect that Absalom would be content with that—after all, what more was there to wish for, once he had been restored to David's good graces?

As it turns out, there was much more that Absalom wished for—he lusted for power and would not be satisfied until he had killed his father and taken the throne for himself. In this study, we will see another tragic element of the Lord's prophecies (which we encountered in Study 5) begin to unfold.

PLAYING POLITICS: *David's son Absalom decides that it's high time he was king, and he sets about building a conspiracy against David.*

1. AFTER THIS: Absalom had fled Jerusalem after murdering Amnon, as we saw in the last study. Joab, the commander of Israel's army, had persuaded David to permit his son to return to Jerusalem, yet David still refused to see him. After two years had passed, Absalom took desperate measures: he had his servants set fire to Joab's crops, forcing Joab to help him gain admission into David's presence. This coercion worked; Joab spoke to David, and the king finally permitted his son to see him again.

ABSALOM PROVIDED HIMSELF WITH CHARIOTS AND HORSES: Absalom began to take on the outward appearance of royalty, driving throughout the land in expensive chariots with men running before him, announcing his approach. He was effectively giving himself a parade whenever he ventured out in public. The Lord had warned the people of Israel that kings would behave in this manner (1 Samuel 8:11).

2. ABSALOM WOULD RISE EARLY: The city gate was the site of public hearings on many civil matters, usually resolved by the city's elders. Such hearings were generally conducted in the early morning hours, before the heat of the day. Absalom deliberately took up a conspicuous position at the city gates in order to set himself up as a sort of judge among the people.

ABSALOM WOULD CALL TO HIM: Absalom went beyond passively standing at the city gates, waiting for people to bring their complaints to him. He deliberately accosted people who were on their way to seek an audience with David.

3. YOUR CASE IS GOOD AND RIGHT: Absalom used flattery to gain the trust of those who had grievances. He did not concern himself with justice, and it appears that he made no effort to look into the validity of anyone's claims. His desire was not for justice, but for power.

THERE IS NO DEPUTY OF THE KING TO HEAR YOU: Absalom then took his plot to another level. He did not stop at offering a sort of drive-through justice, but also told the people that David was too busy to look after his people's concerns. In this way, he planted the early seeds of revolution in the people's minds.

4. OH, THAT I WERE MADE JUDGE IN THE LAND: Here we find an astute political ploy, as Absalom first invented a grievance for the people to hold against David by suggesting that the king was too busy to provide them justice, and then he offered them the solution to that invented grievance. This ploy can still be observed in modern politics.

I would give him justice: In spite of Absalom's wicked intent, there was some truth in his claim of injustice within David's court. The sad irony, of course, was that Absalom had benefited from that very lack of justice, by murdering his brother and getting away with it.

5. he would put out his hand and take him and kiss him: Absalom was essentially running for office, giving himself a parade, making public speeches, offering empty promises, shaking hands—stopping just short of kissing babies. A monarchy, however, is not an elected office. Absalom was deliberately stirring up rebellion against God's king.

Stealing Hearts: *Absalom's tactics bear evil fruit, and he steals the nation's loyalty away from the rightful king. Now it's time to take action.*

6. Absalom stole the hearts of the men of Israel: A national hero will often be said to have won the hearts of the people through great deeds of valor and patriotism. David had won the hearts of Israel through his valor, such as when he defeated Goliath. This is a dire contrast to Absalom's theft of the people's loyalty.

7. after forty years: Other manuscripts translate this "four years." Absalom was probably around thirty years old at this time, and David's entire reign only lasted forty years. This event probably occurred during the final decade of David's rule.

Hebron: Absalom was born in Hebron, and it might have seemed natural to David for his son to return there to fulfill a vow. Its location, about twenty miles south of Jerusalem (see the map in the Introduction), afforded him enough distance from the king to keep his preparations hidden.

11. they went along innocently: Absalom had lured his brothers to a sheepshearing celebration in order to murder Amnon; he had stolen the hearts of the people by playing upon their implicit trust in his integrity when he sat at the city gate; and here he probably selected some of the most influential men in Jerusalem and led them on a sinister errand to Hebron, while they believed it to be a legitimate trip to fulfill a vow to the Lord. This was a characteristic of Absalom's life, to manipulate the people who trusted him.

12. Ahithophel: Bathsheba's grandfather, and one of David's trusted counselors. He would figure significantly later in Absalom's rebellion, and his advice was generally so wise and sound that it "was as if one had inquired at the oracle of God" (2 Samuel 16:23). His decision to side with Absalom was not wise, however, and ultimately led him to a tragic end. It is possible that he was taking revenge upon David for his adultery and murder.

13. The hearts of the men of Israel are with Absalom: This is a sad statement of the fickleness of the human heart. David had done much good for the nation of Israel, and the Lord had blessed His people through his reign—yet they turned against him in an instant, seduced by vain flattery and deception.

14. Arise, and let us flee: David wanted to avoid a bloodbath in the city of Jerusalem, whose very name was connected with the Hebrew word *shalom*, meaning "peace." It was during this time that David wrote Psalm 3: "But You, O Lord, are a shield for me, my glory and the One who lifts up my head. . . . Salvation belongs to the Lord" (v. 3, 8).

16. the king left ten women: David would have assumed that these women would be safe, since Absalom's concern was to kill his father, not his father's concubines. But in leaving them behind, David unwittingly set the stage for the fulfillment of the Lord's prophecies (2 Samuel 12:11), as Absalom used them to disgrace David (2 Samuel 16:20–23).

⌁ Reading 2 Samuel 18:9–18 ⌁

The Death of Absalom: *The conspiracy has led to civil war within Israel, but the Lord's prophecies come to pass with Absalom's tragic death.*

9. Absalom met the servants of David: Much had transpired in the intervening chapters, and open war had erupted between the forces of Absalom and the forces of David.

his head caught in the terebinth: Absalom took great pride in his long, thick hair and in his good looks (2 Samuel 14:25–26), and it is probable that his hair got tangled in the tree's branches. There is a certain irony that what he took pride in should be the cause of his death. The terebinth was a strong, medium-sized tree native to Israel.

hanging between heaven and earth: This poetic phrase describes the literal situation of Absalom, as he was dangling by his hair, but it also suggests the perilous circumstances he had created for himself, as he suddenly found himself without any allies—either on earth or in heaven. Even the very mule that he was riding abandoned him to his fate.

12. Beware lest anyone touch the young man Absalom: David had clearly commanded his three generals (Joab, Abishai, and Ittai) to squelch the rebellion but to not harm his son Absalom. This unnamed soldier was wise to disobey his commander at this point, as Joab insisted that he kill the helpless Absalom. The soldier knew that to do so would be directly against the king's command, and he also realized that Joab would later allow him to take the blame. We will look at Joab more closely in the next study.

15. STRUCK AND KILLED HIM: Despite David's careful insistence that his son be spared, the Lord's prophecy could not be prevented—and his own son died by the sword. Absalom had brought upon himself the judgment of death when he murdered his own brother, and had brought further condemnation by trying to overthrow God's king. Joab disobeyed the king's clear commandment, but on the other hand he brought a quick conclusion to the civil war, preventing further unnecessary deaths—and he also carried out the justice that David had failed to exact, by putting Absalom to death.

18. SET UP A PILLAR FOR HIMSELF: Here is the sad summary of Absalom's life, a young man who had set himself above all others. Saul, another man who was motivated by self-interest, had also set up a monument to himself (1 Samuel 15:12)—and look where it got him.

⌁ First Impressions ⌁

1. *Why did Absalom rebel against his father? What motivated him? How should he have lived his life?*

2. *How might things have been different if David had executed justice after the murder of Amnon? after the rape of Tamar?*

3. Why did the people follow Absalom so readily? What did they hope to gain? Why did they turn their backs on David?

4. Why did Absalom set up a monument to himself? What did this reveal about his character? about his goals?

⤳ SOME KEY PRINCIPLES ⤳

We are to humble ourselves, not to exalt ourselves.

Absalom was a man with immense charisma, renowned for his good looks and magnetic personality. Moreover, he had the best pedigree one could hope for, as his father was a king and his mother was the daughter of a king. He was also gifted politically, and was able to persuade people to his point of view. In short, he had the potential to become a very able leader in Israel.

Yet the great irony of Absalom's life is that by trying to lift himself up, he wound up being cast down. His attitude was the opposite of his father's; David had consistently humbled himself before Saul, even when it put his life in danger. David understood an important principle of God's Word: when God's people humble themselves, God will lift them up.

The world teaches us that if you don't look out for yourself, nobody else will. But God's Word teaches the opposite: Christians don't need to be always looking after their own interests, because we can depend on God to care for us. As James reminds us, "Humble yourselves in the sight of the Lord, and He will lift you up" (James 4:10).

Rebellion against God's king is never ultimately successful.

Absalom probably considered himself to be the heir of David's throne—although that was not God's plan for his life. Absalom was overcome with his desire for power, and that lust led him to take matters into his own hands. He failed to realize that Israel's king was God's chosen servant. If Absalom realized that rebelling against David was as likely to succeed as rebelling against God, his life might have ended in less disgrace.

This was a lesson the Jewish leaders, and specifically Judas, learned in the New Testament. While the Jews were looking for their Messiah, they rejected Jesus because, rather than empowering them, He called them to repentance. Instead of receiving and serving God's king, Judas arranged to have Him killed, and the Jewish leaders were eager to assist. Under God's sovereignty, their very act of treason—the cross—established Jesus' authority and affirmed His kingship, while Judas died a gruesome death (Matthew 27:1–5). Absalom learned the same lesson. By rebelling and overthrowing God's king, he brought about a course of events that ultimately ended with his own death.

Guard your heart against the world's seductions.

One of the most tragic elements of these passages is the ease with which God's people turned against His chosen king. It's not hard to understand from a human perspective, however: Absalom was a charismatic leader who knew how to play politics very skillfully. He played upon people's discontentment and fears, promising them a solution he could not deliver.

The world has not changed since David's day; there are still many forces that play upon our frustrations and desires, making promises that cannot be fulfilled. We find these vain promises in politics, in advertising, in entertainment, and even from some pulpits—promises of temporal wealth, fleshly gratification, personal fulfillment, and much more. The world appeals to our vanity, as Absalom did when he paraded himself through Jerusalem, and it plays upon our fears and dissatisfactions just as Absalom did with those he met at the city gates.

Remember the words David wrote at the very time when his life and kingship were in gravest danger: "Many are they who rise up against me. Many are they who say of me, 'There is no help for him in God.' . . . But You, O LORD, are a shield for me, my glory and the One who lifts up my head" (Psalm 3:1–3). True satisfaction and fulfillment can only be found in God, and what the world promises cannot compare with what He promises.

↶ DIGGING DEEPER ↷

5. *What events led up to Absalom's revolution? What part did David's sin play in setting the stage?*

6. What tactics did Absalom use to gain power? How does the world use those same tactics today to lead people away from God?

7. Why does God command His people to humble themselves? How is this contrary to the world's teachings? How did Jesus demonstrate humility?

8. In practical terms, how does the world try to seduce people away from God today? How can a Christian guard against those seductions?

↳ Taking It Personally ↵

9. Are you trusting the sovereignty of God in your present circumstances, or are you struggling to take control? What Scripture passages might encourage you in this area?

10. In what circumstances are you most tempted to exalt yourself, rather than humble yourself? What can you learn in this regard from the example of Christ?

—§ 8 §—

JOAB

↳ CHARACTER'S BACKGROUND ↲

Joab was a man of action, an experienced soldier who demonstrated courage and strength in battle. He rose to prominence early in David's kingship by leading a decisive victory against the enemy (1 Chronicles 11). He was also an inspiring leader, and the army of Israel was fiercely loyal to his command. While Absalom was devoted to himself, and David was (generally) devoted to the Lord, Joab was devoted to Israel. He did what he thought was best for the nation, regardless of what the Lord, or anyone else, thought about it.

A lifetime of combat tends to make a man very practical in his thinking, and Joab was no exception. He tended to look for the most expedient method of accomplishing his goals, and he pursued those goals with the same fierce zeal that made him excel in battle. He also provided strong counsel at times for the king, such as when he motivated David to overcome his personal grief and show strong leadership to his people.

But every strength brings a corresponding weakness, and Joab's fierce zeal led him to several treacherous murders. In Study 1, we saw a young man named Asahel who courageously ran after Abner, the leader of an army that was rebelling against David early in his reign. Abner tried to persuade Asahel to stop chasing him, but in the end he was compelled to hit him with his spear, killing him on the spot. Asahel was Joab's younger brother, and we will discover in this study that he nurtured a hatred for Abner for many years. When the opportunity presented itself, Joab took revenge.

↳ READING 2 SAMUEL 3:20–30 ↲

A LONG-AWAITED REVENGE: *After years of waiting, Joab hatches an evil plot against Abner—and executes it at the city gate.*

20. ABNER: We now return to the early days of David's reign. This passage immediately follows part of the Scripture reading in Study 1. Abner had been leading the rebellious army on behalf of Ishbosheth, the last son of Saul, but the two men had a disagreement. Abner had just defected to David as this passage opens. It will be important to remember also that Abner had killed a young man in combat named Asahel, Joab's brother. See Study 1 for more information.

21. HE WENT IN PEACE: David had made peace with Abner, even though Abner had been leading the rebellious army against him. David's aim was always to bring peace and unity within Israel, and he was ever ready to forgive those who repented of wrongdoing. Joab was not so forgiving, and it seems he never believed that Abner's change of loyalties was genuine.

22. JOAB CAME FROM A RAID: To gain a balanced picture of Joab, we must also remember that he was a great man of valor, and that he served Israel faithfully throughout David's reign. He was one of the generals who led David's army courageously, going from victory to victory. Still, as we have already seen in Study 4, he was not above performing unscrupulous deeds, as he obeyed David's command to murder Uriah—yet even that wicked deed was done out of obedience to his king. Joab was a man of violence, but he was also faithful to David.

24. WHAT HAVE YOU DONE?: Joab was not shy about confronting David—and his confrontations were often for David's good, as we will see in the next passage. In this case, however, he was motivated by a personal vendetta.

25. ABNER . . . CAME TO DECEIVE YOU: This was not true, although it is quite possible that Joab believed it. It is more likely, however, that Joab was trying to manipulate David in order to gain his own revenge.

27. JOAB TOOK HIM ASIDE IN THE GATE: Joab's trick was the ultimate treachery. First, the city gate was a location of public debate and justice; it was considered a safe place for disputes to be settled. Second, Hebron itself (where this took place) was one of Israel's cities of refuge (Joshua 20), a safe haven for anyone who killed a person accidentally. Joab took advantage of these things to lull Abner into trusting him, then stabbed him in the belly.

FOR THE BLOOD OF ASAHEL HIS BROTHER: Joab did not have a legitimate grievance against Abner. Abner had killed Asahel in combat—and even then he tried very hard to avoid doing so.

29. LET IT REST ON THE HEAD OF JOAB: Once again we find David failing to exact justice in his own household. Joab was guilty of murder, and it was the king's responsibility to put him to death. That sentence was finally carried out by Solomon, as we will see.

⟶ Reading 2 Samuel 19:1–13 ⟵

The Return of the King: *Absalom is dead, at the hands of Joab, commander of David's army. As David, who had fled Jerusalem, prepares to return to his beloved city, he also prepares to oust his commander—for a new one.*

1. THE KING IS WEEPING AND MOURNING FOR ABSALOM: We now move forward to the day of Absalom's death, which we saw in the last study. Rather than being overjoyed at his victory over the rebellion, David was overcome with grief at Absalom's demise. He had commanded Joab to not harm his son, but Joab knew that as long as Absalom was alive, David's throne could not remain secure. Absalom was also deserving of death, both for his brother's murder and for his attempts on his father's life. Joab did not care if what he did was moral. He only seemed to care if it was best for Israel, and in this case he decided that Absalom could not be allowed to live.

3. AS PEOPLE WHO ARE ASHAMED: David's terrific grief over the death of Absalom had a profound effect on his soldiers. They had risked their lives in battle, and many had also been forced to kill their fellow countrymen and perhaps even their own kinsmen in the civil war. They expected their leader to rejoice over the victory, but instead they were filled with shame and dismay.

5. TODAY YOU HAVE DISGRACED ALL YOUR SERVANTS: Once again, we see Joab confronting the king boldly and even aggressively. As usual, Joab may or may not have had David's best interests at heart, but he was concerned for Israel from a political standpoint.

6. YOU LOVE YOUR ENEMIES AND HATE YOUR FRIENDS: Joab could not grasp David's commitment to mercy and unity. David did not desire revenge and bloodshed; he longed for peace and a unified nation—although his application of those priorities was not always wise, such as his failures to enact justice within his household. But Joab did not share David's convictions; his immediate response was always to exact revenge, and he was probably sickened to see his king weeping over a fallen enemy.

IT WOULD HAVE PLEASED YOU WELL: This, of course, was a ridiculous overstatement. David was in a position where he could not avoid catastrophe: either he lost his throne (and his life), or he lost his son.

7. GO OUT AND SPEAK COMFORT TO YOUR SERVANTS: This was sound advice. David needed to honor his loyal soldiers for the cost they had paid in putting down the rebellion. Joab saw clearly that the king risked losing the people's support otherwise. Joab was also making a veiled threat that he would personally see to it that the army defected unless David stopped mourning.

13. Amasa: The leader of Absalom's army.

in place of Joab: David determined to remove Joab from his position as commander of the army because he had killed Absalom, contrary to David's direct orders. In doing this, however, he unwittingly sealed Amasa's fate—for Joab would surely take revenge.

⌁ Reading 2 Samuel 20:1–10 ⌁

A Very Short Career: With Absalom dead, one would think there would be peace in the land. There was not. A rebel comes on the scene and divides the people. War breaks out between the two factions and David gives his first orders to his new commander, Amasa. They will be the last he will ever receive.

1. there happened to be there a rebel: Immediately after the defeat of Absalom, a new division arose between the tribe of Judah and the rest of Israel. Many felt that the people of Judah had been presumptuous in leading David back to Jerusalem in victory; they felt that they should have been included in the victory celebration. It seems a petty quarrel, but there are always people who use minor slights for personal gain. This man Sheba was such a person, and he attempted to use the quarrel to stir up yet another rebellion.

2. every man of Israel deserted David: Yet again we see the tragic fickleness of the human heart.

4. within three days: David needed the army to be reassembled very quickly, because the rebellion by Sheba could become an even worse threat than that of Absalom.

6. Abishai: Joab's older brother.

8. it fell out: Joab's sword undoubtedly slipped from its sheath by design, not by accident.

9. my brother: Joab and Amasa actually were cousins, and this greeting was an open declaration of peaceful intentions. Yet Joab literally betrayed Amasa with a kiss—just as Judas did to Jesus.

⌁ Reading 1 Kings 2:28–34 ⌁

The End of Joab: For years Joab had faithfully and capably served King David as commander of his army. But David, now deceased, had removed him in favor of another, whom Joab in-turn killed. Now, Joab has defected from God's choice to lead Israel, Solomon, to serve Adonijah. It is the last mistake he'll ever make.

28. JOAB HAD DEFECTED TO ADONIJAH: David had died, and his son Solomon had assumed the throne. Adonijah, another son of David, had attempted a rebellion very similar to that of Absalom, and Joab had helped him.

TOOK HOLD OF THE HORNS OF THE ALTAR: Joab could not claim sanctuary in the temple because he was guilty of deliberate murder, not accidental manslaughter.

31. TAKE AWAY . . . THE INNOCENT BLOOD: David, near the end of his life, had charged Solomon to bring justice to Joab (v. 5–6), perhaps regretting his own failure to do so. Here, Solomon finally brought about the death penalty on Joab for the many murders he had committed.

ᕼ FIRST IMPRESSIONS ᕼ

1. *Why did Joab murder Abner? In your opinion, was Abner deserving of death? Was Joab's anger justified?*

2. *What were some of Joab's strengths? What were his weaknesses? Why did his weaknesses gain the upper hand in his life?*

3. Why did Joab kill Absalom? In your opinion, was this justified or unjustified? What were Joab's probable motives?

4. Why did Joab accuse David of loving his enemies and hating his friends? What does this reveal about the character of Joab? about the character of David?

↜ Some Key Principles ↝

Vengeance belongs to God.

The latter part of David's life was plagued by vengeful people. Absalom murdered his brother to get revenge for his sister's rape. Joab murdered two men out of a spirit of vengefulness—and neither man had actually done him any wrong. Yet both murderers undoubtedly justified their crimes in their own minds, convinced that they were accomplishing some "greater good" through their acts of violence. After all, both were avenging some perceived crime against their families—and both stood to gain personally from the deaths of their victims: Absalom removed the heir apparent to David's throne, and Joab removed his competitor for the headship of Israel's army.

It is easy to justify sin in our own minds, but when we do, we fail to see our lives from God's perspective, as we have discussed in previous studies. Absalom may have felt aggrieved that Amnon was not punished for raping Tamar, but it was not his place to even the score. If he had seen the situation through God's eyes, he would have realized that the Lord would address Amnon's guilt in His own time. Absalom was not responsible or qualified to bring justice; only God can do that.

When we take vengeance into our own hands, we only succeed in creating another injustice. Absalom did not amend the situation by addressing Amnon's sin; he only committed another sin—murder. Christians are called to repay evil with righteousness, not to exact justice on those who offend us. "Beloved, do not avenge yourselves," wrote the apostle Paul, "but rather give place to wrath; for it is written, 'Vengeance is Mine, I will repay,' says the Lord. Therefore 'If your enemy is hungry, feed him; if he is thirsty, give him a drink; for in so doing you will heap coals of fire on his head.' Do not be overcome by evil, but overcome evil with good" (Romans 12:19–21).

Man's wrath does not produce God's righteousness.

Joab and Absalom thought they could produce justice and righteousness through their violent acts. Absalom was repaying a sin against his sister, and Joab was keeping David secure in his kingship—or so they reasoned. But their wrathful actions did not produce righteousness; they only produced more sins and more anger.

Anger in itself is not wrong; it is an emotional response to circumstances, and there is a place for righteous wrath. Anger can be an indication that something is wrong in a relationship, and it can alert us to the fact that we need to address an issue with a brother or sister. The danger lies in what we do with our anger, and all too often it leads us into sin.

We are right to be angry at sin and mad at the wickedness in the world around us. But we are wrong when we take out our anger on other people, whether by word or deed. As such, we are warned, "Let every man be . . . slow to wrath; for the wrath of man does not produce the righteousness of God" (James 1:19–20) and further, "'Be angry, [but] do not sin': do not let the sun go down on your wrath" (Ephesians 4:26–27, emphasis added).

Our sin can produce long-term suffering, but God's grace is greater.

We have seen in these studies the dreadful results of David's sin. The Lord declared that David's household would be fraught with treachery and violence, and that terrible prophecy came to pass through the sins of Amnon, Absalom, Joab, and others. David's throne and his very life were threatened by civil strife, power lusts, and revenge—and all these things were a result of his own sins of adultery and murder. One man's sins had a devastating effect upon his entire household, upon the family of Uriah, and on the entire nation of Israel. No one can predict what consequences may follow any act of sin.

Yet this is only part of the truth, as sobering as it is. The other part is equally important: God's grace overcomes the sins of men. David was a sinful man, and his deeds bore bitter fruit for many—yet God still used him to bring about the birth of Jesus Christ. The Lord declared that David's throne would be established forever, as we saw in Study 2, and nothing could prevent God's promise from coming to pass. And, as horrific as David's sins were, the Bible still speaks of him as "a man after [God's] own heart" (Acts 13:22).

This does not give us license to sin, of course, for the consequences of sin are very real, as David's life demonstrates. Yet at the same time, we can rejoice in the fact that the blood of Christ has covered *all* of our sins, and Christians are redeemed from eternal judgment and separation from God. "For as by one man's disobedience many were made sinners, so also by one Man's obedience many will be made righteous. Moreover the law entered that the offense might abound. But where sin abounded, grace abounded much more, so that as sin reigned in death, even so grace might reign through righteousness to eternal life through Jesus Christ our Lord" (Romans 5:19–21).

✎ Digging Deeper ✎

5. *Why did David replace Joab with Amasa? Why did Joab murder Amasa? What do these things reveal about Joab's view of God?*

6. If you had been in Joab's place, how would you have reacted when David replaced you? How would you have felt toward Abner?

7. What are the dangers of someone loving their nation more than they love God? How do you see this in Joab's life?

8. What is righteous anger? When does anger become unrighteous?

9. Are you harboring anger toward another person? What will you do this week to forgive that person? to improve your relationship?

10. In what ways has God demonstrated His grace toward you? How can you imitate Him in your relationships with family, friends, and co-workers?

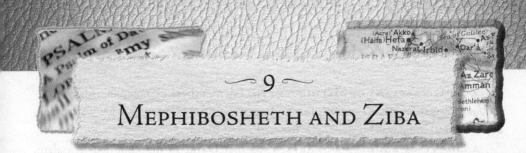

~ 9 ~

MEPHIBOSHETH AND ZIBA

ᴧ CHARACTERS' BACKGROUND ᴧ

We now return to the time when David was forced to flee Jerusalem because of Absalom's rebellion. (See Studies 7 and 8 for more information.) The entire nation of Israel was in chaos; people were fleeing in every direction, and the king was attempting to gather his household and his loyal followers while also trying to end the uprising peacefully. He was bearing a heavy load of grief over the fact that it was his own son who was rebelling against him.

In the midst of all this chaos, David suddenly found himself confronted by Ziba, the steward of Mephibosheth. You will remember from Study 3 that Mephibosheth was Saul's grandson, the son of Jonathan, and David had honored him because of his promise to Jonathan. Most kings would have put him to death in order to avoid any threat to their throne, but David had shown him mercy by letting him live—and had then gone beyond that with a standing invitation to dine at his own table every day. Mephibosheth had much to be grateful for.

But at this point, Ziba came to the king claiming that Mephibosheth had remained in Jerusalem in hopes of becoming king. Ziba presented himself to David as a loyal servant, bearing gifts and promising that his household would follow David wherever he went. Despite some obvious holes in Ziba's story, in the heat of the moment, David did not have the ability to investigate, and he awarded Ziba Mephibosheth's entire estate. It is not until later that Mephibosheth gets the chance to present his own side to the story, and his godly character will be vindicated.

ᴧ READING 2 SAMUEL 16:1–4 ᴧ

ZIBA'S ACCUSATION: *David has fled Jerusalem during Absalom's revolt, and he is met by Ziba, the steward of Mephibosheth's household.*

1. THE TOP OF THE MOUNTAIN: This passage opens as David was fleeing from Absalom's rebellion. He was climbing the Mount of Olives to escape Jerusalem.

Ziba the servant of Mephibosheth: We met these two men in Study 3. Mephibosheth was Jonathan's son, Saul's grandson and only remaining heir. He was lame in both feet, and Ziba was his employee, the steward of his estate.

A couple of saddled donkeys: Ziba met David as the king fled Jerusalem, bringing him a generous gift of food and provisions for David and his men. This was a way of publicly declaring his loyalty to David during the revolution, and on the surface it was a wise act. We will see, however, that Ziba's motives were not pure.

3. where is your master's son: Ziba had been the steward of Saul's properties when Saul was king. Both Saul and Jonathan died on the same day, and the estate went to Saul's grandson Mephibosheth. David was immediately suspicious that Ziba was presenting the gifts without Mephibosheth being present—and this was evidently Ziba's intention. It provided Ziba with the opportunity to betray his employer.

He is staying in Jerusalem: This much was true: Mephibosheth was lame and could not easily escape Jerusalem without help, which Ziba apparently refused to provide him.

Israel will restore the kingdom of my father to me: This accusation, however, was false. Ziba was telling David that Mephibosheth had taken advantage of Absalom's revolt to attempt a coup of his own. As Saul's only remaining heir, he might have thought that he could ascend the throne himself. We will see that he had no such designs.

4. all that belongs to Mephibosheth is yours: One can hardly fault David for making this rash judgment. The moment Absalom raised himself in rebellion, more than half the nation turned against David. The king found himself betrayed by many of his most loyal supporters. Ziba's accusation also sounded plausible in the heat of the moment.

That I may find favor in your sight: This was a true statement on Ziba's part. His entire motivation was to seize for himself the lands of Mephibosheth, and he was taking advantage of the rebellion for his own gain.

✍ Reading 2 Samuel 19:24–30 ✍

Mephibosheth's Rebuttal: *David has returned to Jerusalem after the death of Absalom, and he is met this time by Mephibosheth—who has a different account of the affair.*

24. MEPHIBOSHETH THE SON OF SAUL CAME DOWN TO MEET THE KING: We now move forward to the time following Absalom's death, when David was returning to Jerusalem. Mephibosheth was actually Saul's grandson, the son of Jonathan.

HE HAD NOT CARED FOR HIS FEET: Mephibosheth was an invalid, and may have required assistance in some of his personal care. But his disheveled appearance was about far more than having no servants to help him; he had deliberately neglected his outward appearance as a sign of his grief over David's suffering.

25. WHY DID YOU NOT GO WITH ME: Those who had remained loyal to David had fled Jerusalem with him. Anyone who remained in the city was immediately suspected of disloyalty. David's question was thus quite valid.

26. BECAUSE YOUR SERVANT IS LAME: Ziba's lie began to be exposed. Mephibosheth had intended to ride to David on a donkey, but Ziba took advantage of his disability to ride out ahead of him, bearing the false report.

28. ALL MY FATHER'S HOUSE WERE BUT DEAD MEN: All of Saul's family were dead except Mephibosheth, so this was certainly accurate on a literal level. But Mephibosheth was referring to the fact that, under any other king, his own life would have been forfeit. As we saw in Study 3, David had done something quite extraordinary in the world's eyes when he honored the grandson of the previous king. Ordinarily, the king would put to death the heirs of his rival in order to guard against rebellion.

WHAT RIGHT HAVE I: Mephibosheth's gratitude seems genuine. He recognized that he had received great grace from the king, and that he had no grounds for demanding anything further.

29. WHY DO YOU SPEAK ANYMORE OF YOUR MATTERS? : In other words, "I give up! This is too complicated for me to sort out right now." David was overcome with grief over the death of Absalom, he was faced with reestablishing his throne after the rebellion, and he had countless people demanding his attention. He may also have seen that his previous decision to give the lands to Ziba was hasty, since he had not investigated the charges. With all that was going on, Mephibosheth's estate must have seemed rather insignificant to David at that moment.

YOU AND ZIBA DIVIDE THE LAND: David did not have time to investigate the truth of these conflicting accusations, and he was probably concerned that he not overreact in either direction. It probably seemed more sensible under the circumstances to allow Mephibosheth and Ziba to resolve the dispute themselves. If Mephibosheth was telling the truth, however, the decision was unjust—Ziba should have been punished for his false accusation, and Mephibosheth should have remained in possession of what was rightfully his.

30. LET HIM TAKE IT ALL: At this point, the truth of Mephibosheth's story became clear. He was not motivated by a desire for personal gain, as Ziba had been—in fact, he had little concern for his own possessions. His chief desire was to remain in the presence of the king, and he was content to forgive Ziba's treachery and let him keep his heart's desire. David's son Solomon would later execute a very similar judgment in a dispute between two prostitutes who each claimed that a baby was her own. Solomon offered to cut the baby in two, and the true mother was so horrified at the prospect that she immediately volunteered to give the child to her rival (1 Kings 3:16–28).

∽ First Impressions ∾

1. *If you had been in David's position, how would you have responded to Ziba's accusations against Mephibosheth?*

2. *If you had been in David's position, how would you have responded to Mephibosheth's claims upon returning to Jerusalem?*

3. *What evidence is there that Mephibosheth was telling the truth and Ziba was lying?*

4. *If you had been in Mephibosheth's position, how would you have dealt with Ziba's treachery?*

⌁ Some Key Principles ⌁

Do not be ungrateful.

Ziba had experienced much blessing in his life. He had been entrusted by King Saul to oversee all the king's lands and possessions, a position that gave him great power and authority. It also gave him significant personal wealth, as his own household had grown to be quite large (2 Samuel 9:10). The death of Saul, however, could easily have ruined him—might even have put his own life in danger. But David's generosity toward the house of Saul enabled him to retain his wealth and remain in his position of steward over Mephibosheth's inheritance. Yet Ziba was an opportunist: rather than being grateful for these blessings, he sought to gain still more through treachery and guile.

Mephibosheth, in contrast, recognized that he was entitled only to death. The fact that he was Saul's only remaining heir would have been a death sentence under any other king, yet David had gone beyond merely allowing him to live by inviting him to dine at the king's table every day—a very high honor. Mephibosheth responded to David's kindness with love and loyalty; his grief was quite genuine over David's banishment from Jerusalem, and his joy was evident upon the king's return.

Christians are in the same position as Mephibosheth. We are all sinners, entitled to nothing but the death sentence from a holy and just God. Yet God has gone far beyond merely forgiving us of our sins and commuting the death sentence—He has also made us children of God and heirs with Christ, inviting us to commune with Him freely, both now and through eternity. When we are tempted to think that life owes us more, it is time to take stock of all God has provided to us through His Son. A thankful spirit will protect us from a spirit of ingratitude.

We are commanded to forgive those who wrong us.

Ziba committed a gross act of treachery against his employer. He was an opportunist, and he saw a golden opportunity to advance himself in the eyes of the king while also increasing his own wealth and power. It didn't matter to him that he had to slander the name of Mephibosheth in the process. In fact, he was effectively condemning Mephibosheth to death by his false accusation, since the king would have been within his rights to execute those who had joined in the rebellion.

Mephibosheth, however, did not try to get even with his accuser. Ziba had falsely accused him of a crime deserving death, and Mephibosheth would have been fully justified in demanding that Ziba be put to death instead. At the very least, he could have demanded that all his lands and possessions be returned to him, since they had been taken away by treachery. But Mephibosheth chose instead to forgive Ziba—indeed, he went beyond forgiveness by giving him all the possessions that Ziba had coveted in the first place.

These actions demonstrated that Mephibosheth's highest priority was to be in fellowship with the king. His attitude was that he didn't deserve those possessions in the first place, because he rightly deserved death—and that attitude made it easy for him to forgive another man who also deserved death. In this, Mephibosheth demonstrated the principle taught by Jesus: "If you forgive men their trespasses, your heavenly Father will also forgive you. But if you do not forgive men their trespasses, neither will your Father forgive your trespasses" (Matthew 6:14–15).

Don't judge without all of the information.

David was fleeing Jerusalem with his life in danger. As king, he was directly respon-sible for the welfare of those who remained loyal to him, and he also had to be formu-lating plans on how to counteract Absalom's rebellion. He was being assailed as he fled by many people with many concerns, and he had to make quick decisions to send some ahead, some back, some into enemy territory.

It is easy to understand that he made some decisions hastily, and certainly his de-cision concerning Mephibosheth's lands is an example. But that decision proved to be unjust; it would have been far wiser for David to postpone a judgment until he had the leisure to look into the facts behind Ziba's accusation. The results of this hasty decision could have been even worse, since Mephibosheth could have faced the death penalty for such treachery if Ziba's claims had proven true.

Proverbs 18:17 says, "The first one to plead his case seems right, until his neighbor comes and examines him." When a person presents his case to another, he always pres-ents it in the most favorable way, so that the one listening is convinced. But usually when the other side of the case is heard, the truth comes to light. For this reason, it is always wiser to postpone decision making until we've had time to consult both sides of an issue, and to seek the Lord in prayer. Not only does God's grace overcome our human frailties but He has also promised to give wisdom whenever we ask. As James reminds us, "If any of you lacks wisdom, let him ask of God, who gives to all liberally and without reproach, and it will be given to him" (James 1:5).

ᨈ DIGGING DEEPER ᨈ

5. Why did Mephibosheth give all his property to Ziba? What does this reveal about his priorities?

6. Why did Ziba tell this lie in the first place? What did he hope to gain? What does this reveal about his priorities?

7. What led David to make unjust decisions? How might he have handled this situation differently?

8. In what ways does Mephibosheth illustrate Christlike character? How do his actions serve as example for Christian gratitude?

☙ Taking It Personally ☙

9. What decisions in your life require wisdom at present? What steps will you take to ensure that you make a wise decision?

10. Make a list below of things you are grateful for; then spend time giving thanks to God for His love and generosity.

SECTION 3:

THEMES

In This Section:

OBEDIENCE AND BLESSING

2 SAMUEL 6

~ THEMATIC BACKGROUND ~

When the Israelites were leaving Egypt and heading toward the promised land, the Lord instructed them to create a movable tabernacle for worship. He was very explicit on all the details of that tabernacle—on its construction, on the materials to be used, and on the many articles to be contained in it. One of those articles was the ark of the covenant, an ornate chest containing the tablets of the law and other sacred objects. On top of the ark were two cherubim, carved representations of angels bowed low with their wingtips touching. This ark was the symbol of God's presence with His people.

The Lord also gave explicit instructions on how the ark was to be moved. It had rings on the sides, through which long wooden poles were slipped for carrying. Only the Levites (priests from the tribe of Levi) were permitted to move the ark, and they were to balance the wooden poles on their shoulders with the ark in the midst. Nobody was permitted to touch the ark at any time, because it represented the physical presence of God, and God cannot tolerate sin in His presence.

Saul's army had carried the ark into battle against the Philistines, but the presence of God was no longer with Saul, and the ark had been captured by the enemy. The Philistines carried it back to one of their cities and placed it in a pagan temple, at the feet of an idol. This was their way of demonstrating that their god Dagon had defeated the God of Israel—but the Lord quickly let them know they were wrong. Disease and death swept through their cities, and the Philistines decided to return the ark to Israel. They had no knowledge, however, of God's instructions on how to move it, so they placed it on an oxcart and sent it away.

In this study, we will learn that God loves to bless His people—but He also demands that His people obey His instructions. There are no excuses for violating God's holiness, and David would learn this lesson the hard way.

⟆ READING 2 SAMUEL 6:1–23 ⟆

REMEMBERING THE ARK: *The ark of the covenant belonged in Jerusalem, but it had been in Kirjath Jearim for many years. David leads the people to bring it back.*

1. DAVID GATHERED ALL THE CHOICE MEN OF ISRAEL: We return once more to the early days of David's reign. David's desire to move the ark surrounded by the most prominent people of Israel, rather than by using Levites as the Law commanded, was a direct disobedience of the Lord's directions for moving the ark. According to 1 Chronicles 13:4, the choice to use prominent men was made because it was thought to be "right in the eyes of all the people."

2. BAALE JUDAH: That is, Kirjath Jearim, about ten miles west of Jerusalem. See the map in the Introduction.

THE ARK OF GOD: The ark of the covenant was a sacred article in the tabernacle. It represented the dwelling place of God among His people. The armies of Saul had carried the ark into battle many years earlier, but it had been captured by the Philistines. They had placed it in a pagan temple, but the Lord had sent plagues against their people. The Philistines had then returned the ark to Israel, and it had remained in Kirjath Jearim (1 Samuel 4–6). See the previous book in this series, *Prophets, Priests, and Kings*, for further information.

WHO DWELLS BETWEEN THE CHERUBIM: The ark featured two sculptured angels, or cherubim, seated on its top. The Lord was said to dwell between the cherubim because the ark itself represented His presence in Israel.

IMITATING THE PHILISTINES: *The people disregard God's clear instructions on how to carry the ark, placing it instead on an oxcart. They learned this technique from the Philistines.*

3. A NEW CART: The Lord had given strict directives to the people of Israel on how to transport the ark. It was to be moved only by descendants of Kohath, members of the tribe of Levi (Numbers 3:30–31), and it was to be carried on poles designed for that purpose (Exodus 25:12–14). The Philistines, however, had returned the ark to Israel by oxcart, and David was evidently imitating their example.

5. THE HOUSE OF ISRAEL PLAYED MUSIC BEFORE THE LORD: Literally, they "made merry" before the Lord. The entire event was turning into more of a parade than an act of worship. Thousands of Israelites had lined the street, while those politically connected to David (rather than the priests) surrounded the ark. The return of the ark to Jerusalem, where it belonged, was to be a joyous event for the people of Israel—and it undoubtedly would have been, if they had simply followed the Lord's directions on how to move it.

6. TOOK HOLD OF IT: Uzzah's motivation was good; the oxen had stumbled, and the ark began to totter on the cart. But man's good intentions do not excuse disobedience to God's Word. The sad fact is that David's failure to lead the people according to God's directions caused an innocent man to lose his life.

7. GOD STRUCK HIM THERE FOR HIS ERROR: God had clearly warned the people that they were not permitted to touch the ark or any of the holy things in the tabernacle, lest they be struck dead (Numbers 4:15). God cannot tolerate sin in His presence; not even the high priest was exempt from these instructions.

8. DAVID BECAME ANGRY: God's anger was aroused by man's sinful presumption in disregarding His clear commands, but David's anger was aroused by God's justice. His anger would have been better turned against himself, as he had led the people in this error.

PEREZ UZZAH: That is, *outbreak against Uzzah.*

9. DAVID WAS AFRAID OF THE LORD: There is a "fear of the Lord" that is a healthy respect for His character and holiness, and fear of God's justice and wrath can move a person toward repentance of sin and salvation. Yet Christians have been saved from the wrath of God, and we should never be afraid to enter His presence. When we do sin, we should not tremble in fear of God's punishment, but rather we should immediately confess the sin and restore our relationship with Him (1 John 1:9). David's fear, however, was brought about by his own sin. Rather than trembling, he should have confessed that sin and set about carrying the ark back to Jerusalem in the correct manner. It was this type of fear that drove Adam and Eve into hiding when the Lord walked in the garden of Eden after they sinned (Genesis 3).

10. DAVID WOULD NOT MOVE THE ARK OF THE LORD: Unconfessed sin can freeze a person in his tracks, hindering his continued ministry for the Lord. David would not resume this good task until he had dealt with his guilt.

OBEYING GOD'S WORD: *The people set out to return the ark a second time, but this time they do it in the manner God commanded.*

11. THE LORD BLESSED OBED-EDOM AND ALL HIS HOUSEHOLD: Apparently Obed-Edom feared God and honored Him by honoring the ark. God responded by blessing his household.

12. SO DAVID WENT AND BROUGHT UP THE ARK: When David was told that the Lord had blessed the household of Obed-Edom, he recognized that God did not desire to rain down judgment and wrath upon His people—He desired to bless them. It is important for God's people to remember this, as it can help us to be quick in confessing sin and restoring our relationship with Him. Once David had remembered the love of God, he was quick to restore the ark "with gladness."

13. THOSE BEARING THE ARK: This time, the people of Israel carried the ark in the correct manner, bearing it upon the shoulders of the Levites rather than trundling it along in an oxcart.

DANCING BEFORE THE LORD: *David leads the people into Jerusalem, dancing with joy in the presence of the Lord. His wife, however, is not pleased.*

14. DAVID DANCED BEFORE THE LORD: The people were overjoyed at restoring the ark to its rightful place in Jerusalem, and they expressed that joy with all their might. Here, dancing was an act of worship; David's dancing was an expression of joy in the presence of the Lord and His ark.

16. MICHAL: The daughter of Saul, and David's first wife. Saul had given her in marriage to David after he slew two hundred Philistines (1 Samuel 18).

SHE DESPISED HIM IN HER HEART: Michal did not share David's overwhelming joy at being in God's presence; she evidently set a higher priority upon decorum and kingly dignity.

18. HE BLESSED THE PEOPLE IN THE NAME OF THE LORD OF HOSTS: Notice the repetition of David's blessings, as he blessed the people and then returned to bless his own household (v. 20). Earlier he had been filled with fear in the presence of God, but once he had resumed his obedience to the Lord's commands, his fear was turned to blessing. Obedience to God always brings great blessings, and those blessings overflow to others.

20. UNCOVERING HIMSELF: David did not expose himself in any indecent manner. Michal evidently was appalled to see the king dancing with joy, wearing the ephod (the humble clothes of a priest) rather than elegant royal robes. She felt that David had somehow debased himself with his open expression of joy and worship.

21. IT WAS BEFORE THE LORD: David responded to Michal's accusation by pointing out that he was dancing not for the benefit of the people around him but for the glory of God—it was an act of worship, not a public display.

22. I WILL BE EVEN MORE UNDIGNIFIED THAN THIS: David was not concerned about his public image or about appearing dignified and aloof as king. He saw himself through the eyes of God, and that kept him humble in his own sight.

∼ First Impressions ∼

1. Why did David choose prominent people to move the ark? Why didn't he use Levites? Why do you think they used an oxcart to begin with?

2. Why did God strike down Uzzah? If you had been Uzzah, what would you have done when you saw the ark teetering?

3. Compare the two attempts at moving the ark. What was different, and what was the same?

4.   *Why did Michal become angry with David? If you had been in her position, how would you have responded to the king's dancing?*

ᔊ Some Key Principles ᔊ

God is to be worshiped in His prescribed way.

The Lord had given strict instructions to Israel on how to carry the ark. They were to carry it on long poles balanced on their shoulders. No one was allowed to touch it, because it represented the presence of a holy God who cannot tolerate sin. Instead, the people carried the ark on an oxcart. David had probably gotten this idea from the Philistines, who had returned the ark to Israel in just such a cart. The Philistines, however, did not know the commands of God—they invented their methods based on what they thought would please a pagan deity.

The Lord not only said *how* the ark was supposed to be moved but *who* was supposed to move it. A particular family of Levites was supposed to oversee the ark's transportation. When David first tried to move the ark, he disobeyed this directive and replaced the Levite priests with the prominent political leaders of Israel. With happy music being played, drawing further attention to the blatant disobedience of God's commands, the whole event had become a parade. And the people of Israel knew better—they had the Word of God to lead them, and they were accountable to obey it.

God cannot be worshiped using whatever means are most appealing or acceptable to the world. John 4:24 says that those who worship God must "worship him in spirit and in truth." People must worship not simply by external conformity to religious rituals; they must worship based on the truth of God's Word and with a Spirit that longs to obey His commands. If the proper heart attitude is absent, worship is false.

The Lord is eager to bless, not to punish.

David was filled with fear of God's anger when he failed to follow the Lord's prescribed method of carrying the ark, and that fear hindered his ministry. But the Lord was not looking for excuses to display His wrath; He was eager to bless the people and to lead them into righteousness and obedience. He poured out blessings upon the household of Obed-Edom just as He longed to do for the entire nation of Israel.

Our sin can cause us to have an inaccurate perspective of God's character. We can fall into the error of thinking that God is an angry Being who looks for shortcomings and failures in the lives of His people, eager to punish and rebuke them. The truth is just the opposite: the Lord longs to bless His people, and He is always looking for ways to demonstrate His love toward us.

The ultimate example of this is found in Christ. If God had been eager to punish, He might have simply condemned the entire human race to eternal punishment, since that is precisely what our sins deserved. But He sent His own Son expressly to die on the cross to pay the penalty for those sins, enabling us to be restored to fellowship with Him. As David himself wrote, "The LORD is merciful and gracious, slow to anger, and abounding in mercy. He will not always strive with us, nor will He keep His anger forever. He has not dealt with us according to our sins, nor punished us according to our iniquities" (Psalm 103:8–10).

It's good to pour out our worship before the Lord.

David danced before the Lord, leaping and whirling in an open expression of joy. He was the king of Israel, one of the most powerful leaders in the world at the time, and his position certainly required times of sober dignity. Yet he was also the leader of God's people, and it was in that capacity that he led them in a joyful demonstration of their love for God.

The people had good reason for such joy. They were bringing the ark back to Jerusalem, and the ark itself was a symbol of the fact that the Creator of the universe had chosen to make His dwelling among them. Of course, the ark was just a *symbol* of God's presence; He did not physically dwell in it, and the people were restricted in their intimacy with God. Christians today have something much more precious: we have the Holy Spirit of God dwelling inside us, and nothing could be more intimate than that!

We have good reason for rejoicing as believers in Christ Jesus, for we have intimate access to the presence of God at all times. We should be quick to emulate David's example, expressing our joy before the Lord in blissful praise and worship. "Be filled with the Spirit," wrote the apostle Paul, "speaking to one another in psalms and hymns and spiritual songs, singing and making melody in your heart to the Lord, giving thanks always for all things to God the Father in the name of our Lord Jesus Christ" (Ephesians 5:18–20).

∽ DIGGING DEEPER ∽

5. What does this passage reveal about the character of God? about the importance of obedience?

6. How did you react when you read of God's punishment on Uzzah? How did David react? What do our human responses reveal about our understanding of God's Word?

7. To what extent was David responsible for the death of Uzzah? To what extent was Uzzah responsible? How might this tragedy have been avoided?

8. Why did the Israelites imitate the Philistine's method for moving the ark? Why is imitation more appealing to some people than conforming to God's Word?

୬ TAKING IT PERSONALLY ୬

9. Do you tend to view God as eager to punish, or eager to bless? How does one's view of God affect one's behavior?

10. List some reasons for rejoicing in your own life; then spend time in praise and worship to the Lord.

THE MAN AFTER GOD'S OWN HEART

~ THEMATIC BACKGROUND ~

In these studies, we have seen David commit some grievous sins, and we have witnessed the terrible results of those offenses. He committed adultery with Bathsheba; he murdered Uriah; he even tried to cover up those sins and continue on with his life as though he'd done nothing wrong. And yet God described David as "a man after My own heart" (Acts 13:22; see also 1 Samuel 13:14).

At first glance, this seems like a tremendous contradiction. How can a murderer and adulterer be a man after God's own heart? In order to understand this, we must look at David's whole life, not merely at a certain season of sin. We must also remember that all people sin—including Christians, who have the Holy Spirit living within them.

In this study, we will address this question, and we will let David speak for himself. We will look at two psalms that he wrote—one written soon after he was confronted by Nathan, the other composed in thanksgiving for God's great salvation. We will discover that David's heart was always turned toward the Lord, and that he was eager to restore his relationship with God after his sin. In this, we will learn that anyone can be a person after God's own heart by keeping God first in all areas of our lives.

~ READING PSALM 51:1–19 ~

A CRY FOR MERCY: *David is confronted by Nathan concerning his sin with Bathsheba, and he immediately throws himself at the feet of God.*

HEADING TO PSALM 51: David wrote this psalm after he was challenged by Nathan over his sin with Bathsheba and the subsequent murder of her husband (see Study 4). It is called a *penitential psalm* because the author is repentant for his sins. (Other penitential psalms include Psalms 6; 32; 38; 102; 130; and 143.)

1. Have mercy upon me: In this cry, David was confessing that he was guilty as charged, and he offered no excuses. He recognized that he was entirely deserving of the Lord's just anger, and all he could do was ask for mercy.

According to Your lovingkindness: David acknowledged that God was under no obligation to extend mercy, and that any mercy he was shown would flow naturally out of God's own kindness and generosity. It is significant to note that David was not asking God to be kind—he understood that God *is* kind and loving. There is a sense of expectation in this psalm, as David's pleas for forgiveness were seasoned with the anticipation that his loving God would grant it.

Blot out my transgressions: This image is of a written record of David's deeds, which God completely expunged, erasing the sin so completely that it was as clean as if it had never been written in the first place. Elsewhere, David used a similar metaphor: "As far as the east is from the west, so far has He removed our transgressions from us" (Psalm 103:12).

2. Wash me thoroughly: David recognized that sin defiled him, making him filthy and unfit to approach God's presence. He knew there was nothing he could do to cleanse himself; cleansing could only come from the hand of God. Yet again we get the sense of expectation that God will do it.

Confessing His Sins: *David does not try to explain away his guilt; instead, he confesses openly that he has sinned.*

---

3. I acknowledge my transgressions: When Nathan confronted David concerning his sin, David instantly acknowledged the truth of the accusation: "I have sinned against the Lord" (2 Samuel 12:13).

my sin is always before me: This expresses beautifully the oppressive weight of guilt and remorse that a person experiences with unconfessed sin.

4. Against You, You only, have I sinned: This is an important concept to understand: all sin is ultimately committed against God. David's sins damaged many people—indeed, the entire nation of Israel—but the final offense was to God. Joseph recognized the same principle when he was being tempted to commit adultery: "How then can I do this great wickedness, and sin against God?" he asked the temptress (Genesis 39:9).

done this evil in Your sight: David had tried to pretend for many months that the Lord didn't see his sin, but in his repentance he came to acknowledge that nothing is hidden from God.

5. IN SIN MY MOTHER CONCEIVED ME: David's sin was not some rare occurrence that caught him by surprise. On the contrary, he realized that he was a sinner from birth, and that sin was part of his basic human nature. Everyone who has ever lived has sinned, because everyone is descended from Adam—everyone, that is, except Jesus. The apostle Paul confirmed this. He wrote, "For all have sinned and fall short of the glory of God" (Romans 3:23).

6. YOU DESIRE TRUTH IN THE INWARD PARTS: That is, in the inner man, the true nature of a person's character—that which is hidden from others but visible to God. "Truth in the inward parts" can only be produced by staying in God's Word. His truth searches a man's inmost being, cutting through all pretense and self-deception and bringing light and life. "For the word of God is living and powerful," wrote the author of Hebrews, "and sharper than any two-edged sword, piercing even to the division of soul and spirit, and of joints and marrow, and is a discerner of the thoughts and intents of the heart" (4:12).

7. HYSSOP: An aromatic plant used by the priests to sprinkle blood or water on a person during ceremonial cleansing (Leviticus 14:6). David was yearning for a complete cleansing from the defilement of his sin.

A PRAYER FOR RESTORATION: *David's concern is not that he will suffer punishment, but that he is out of fellowship with God. His desire is to be restored.*

---

8. MAKE ME HEAR JOY AND GLADNESS: Here is another beautiful description of the deadening effect sin has upon a person's spirit. All joy goes out of life; things that once brought pleasure or satisfaction no longer do so.

THE BONES YOU HAVE BROKEN: David's guilt was causing him extreme anguish, even to the point of physical symptoms. He also wrote of this experience, "When I kept silent, my bones grew old through my groaning all the day long. For day and night Your hand was heavy upon me; my vitality was turned into the drought of summer" (Psalm 32:3–4).

9. HIDE YOUR FACE FROM MY SINS: God cannot tolerate the presence of sin, as we have seen throughout these studies. To hide His face is to turn His back on sin, and David wanted his sin to be so utterly eradicated that even God would never look upon it again. The opposite of this—when God turns His face away from the unrepentant sinner who refuses His offer of forgiveness—is horrible. The prophet Isaiah wrote, "Behold, the LORD's hand is not shortened, that it cannot save; nor His ear heavy, that it cannot hear. But your iniquities have separated you from your God; and your sins have hidden His face from you, so that *He will not hear*" (Isaiah 59:1–2, emphasis added). The Lord is always working to bring sinners to repentance, and He will never turn His face away from the one who confesses sin—but the day will come when He will turn His back forever on those who have rejected Him.

10. CREATE IN ME A CLEAN HEART: The word translated *create* is the same word used in Genesis 1:1, "In the beginning God created the heavens and the earth." David recognized that a pure heart was something that only God could create; he could not produce it himself. Man's heart is indelibly defiled with sin, and humanity is powerless to change that. A pure heart does not naturally evolve in any man or woman; neither can anyone create it. Such a transformation can only come from God.

11. DO NOT CAST ME AWAY FROM YOUR PRESENCE: The Lord gave Israel's leaders His Spirit, empowering them to deliver His people from their enemies. But when God's kings or judges rejected His leadership, He took His Spirit away from them. The Lord had rejected Saul as king and had removed His Spirit from him (1 Samuel 16:14). The same fate befell Samson (Judges 16:20). But Christians will never experience either God's rejection or the removal of the Holy Spirit. We are permanently sealed in Christ, and the Holy Spirit is our guarantee of eternal life (2 Corinthians 1:21–22).

13. I WILL TEACH TRANSGRESSORS YOUR WAYS: David was learning from personal experience about the character of God and the nature of sin. His sin could not be hidden from God, and it separated him from His presence—yet the Lord was eager and quick to forgive that sin the moment it was confessed. This glorious news brought joy and restoration to David, and it was only natural that he would want to share it with others.

14. DELIVER ME FROM THE GUILT OF BLOODSHED: The Lord did this the moment David confessed his sin (2 Samuel 12:13).

17. THE SACRIFICES OF GOD ARE A BROKEN SPIRIT: God did accept men's sacrifices in the Old Testament, but only when they were accompanied by genuine repentance. God delights in the restored sinner rather than in the sacrificial offering; it is the *result* of the sacrifice—the restored relationship with His people—that brings God pleasure.

⌇ READING 2 SAMUEL 22:1–51 ⌇

GOD MY DELIVERER: *David praises the Lord for His protection and deliverance, time and time again. He places his security in the fortress of God's love.*

1. THE LORD HAD DELIVERED HIM FROM THE HAND OF ALL HIS ENEMIES: David may have written this psalm toward the end of his life, after the Lord had given him victory over the Philistines and other enemies of Israel, although some scholars date it earlier in his reign. It is very similar to Psalm 18.

2. The Lord is my rock: The rock is used as a metaphor of the Lord throughout Scripture. It depicts something solid, immovable, and unchanging, a stable anchor amid life's storms. Jesus is also pictured as the cornerstone on which the kingdom of God is built (1 Peter 2:6), as well as a stone of stumbling (1 Peter 2:8).

my fortress and my deliverer: The major theme of this psalm is David's praise to God for delivering him repeatedly from his enemies. God had been a consistent defender, a safe place of refuge throughout David's tumultuous life.

4. I will call upon the Lord: This was a characteristic of David's life, calling upon the Lord in all circumstances. He called upon God after he sinned, as we saw in the previous psalm, and he called upon Him in praise and adoration, as we see here.

7. In my distress I called upon the Lord: David also called upon the Lord when he needed help and strength.

He heard my voice: In all his calling to the Lord, David was always confident that he was heard—and he was never disappointed.

8. He was angry: This picture of God's wrath is both terrifying and accurate (Revelation 19:11–21). But David also recognized that he would not face that fury, and Christians can rest in the assurance that we, too, will never face the wrathful judgment of God.

The Character of God: *David praises God for who He is, rejoicing in His perfect character.*

---

17. He sent from above: Jesus literally fulfilled this picture when He descended from heaven and took on human form in order to redeem His people from death—the strongest of man's enemies.

20. He delivered me because He delighted in me: David was not suggesting that he was worthy of God's favor, but that God delivered him simply because He chose to, and He delighted in him because He is a God of love.

21. The Lord rewarded me according to my righteousness: David was not claiming that he was inherently righteous or free from sin; indeed, if he wrote this psalm later in his life, he was well aware of his sinful nature, as we saw in Psalm 51. The righteousness of which he was speaking was his basic desire to obey God's Word. He had a heart to please God, and the Lord was faithful to bless him.

22. I have kept the ways of the Lord: Here is another element of being a man after God's own heart: obedience. David certainly committed sin, but his life overall was characterized by faithfulness to God's directions.

23. ALL HIS JUDGMENTS WERE BEFORE ME: The man after God's own heart will spend time on a regular basis studying God's Word.

24. I WAS ALSO BLAMELESS BEFORE HIM: This does not mean that David never sinned—it means that his sins were forgiven and removed from the record, blotted out. When we confess our sins, God always forgives them—blots them out and eliminates them from His mind. Christians still miss the mark, but our sins are completely covered by the blood of Christ, and God sees us through that blood as righteous before Him.

26. WITH THE MERCIFUL YOU WILL SHOW YOURSELF MERCIFUL: The righteousness of man does not earn God's favor. Rather, He is always working to lead men into righteousness. He encourages mercy and humility, because those are His own characteristics, and He resists ungodly behavior in an attempt to move sinners toward Himself.

28. YOUR EYES ARE ON THE HAUGHTY: God seeks to "bring them down" not because He is looking for an excuse to judge, but because He wants the proud man to humble himself before God.

36. THE SHIELD OF YOUR SALVATION: This description summarizes all that God is to His people, saving us from eternal judgment and protecting us from the enemy of our souls.

⤳ FIRST IMPRESSIONS ⤳

1. *On what basis did David hope to find mercy from God? Why was he so confident of receiving it?*

2. *What did David mean when he said, "In sin my mother conceived me" (Psalm 51:5)? What does this teach about human nature? about God's nature?*

3. What did David mean when he said that God "desire[s] truth in the inward parts" (Psalm 51:6)? What does this teach about the character of God?

4. According to the passage from 2 Samuel, why did God deliver David from his enemies? Why did God show His wrath to those people?

ᔐ Some Key Principles ᔐ

When we confess our sins, God utterly blots them out.

David's sins against God were dreadful, ordering the murder of an innocent man (after sleeping with the man's wife), and then trying to hide it from God and others. These offenses brought judgment upon his entire household, and they further resulted in sowing discord and rebellion within his kingdom. God's law demanded the death penalty for both adultery and murder, and David was condemned twice over. Yet God did not put him to death; instead, He "put away" David's sin and blotted it out of existence. David still faced temporal consequences of those sins, but he was set completely free from the judgment and wrath of God.

But God did not show David such grace and mercy until he repented of his sins. David thought he could hide his sin, and for many months he went about his life as though he had done nothing wrong. During that time, however, he was not at peace. "When I kept silent," he wrote, "my bones grew old through my groaning all the day long. For day and night Your hand was heavy upon me; my vitality was turned into the drought of summer" (Psalm 32:3–4). Yet the moment he confessed his sin and repented, he found peace and restoration with God.

The Lord, speaking through the prophet Jeremiah, said of His people, "I will forgive their iniquity, and their sin I will remember no more" (Jeremiah 31:34). God desires unbroken fellowship with all people, and He is quick to forget our trespasses. The important element in this, however, is that God's people should also be quick to confess their sins. "If we confess our sins, He is faithful and just to forgive us our sins and to cleanse us from all unrighteousness" (1 John 1:9).

Christians may face discipline, but we will never face God's angry judgment.

The wrathful judgment of God refers to His ultimate sentence of eternal separation from Himself. This sentence falls upon any who die in their sin, because God cannot tolerate sin in His presence. The Bible teaches that all people have sinned, and that no one can eradicate the sin nature. We are all descended from Adam, and therefore we all share Adam's sinful nature—there is nothing we can do to remove that likeness.

The good news, however, is that what we cannot do, God can! He sent His Son to become a man, born of the Spirit of God. He was not subject to death because He had never sinned, yet He willingly died on the cross in order to pay the penalty for *our* sins. When we accept Christ's atonement for our sins, we are born again into the family of God—and nothing can ever remove us from that family.

The Lord does discipline us in order to produce godly character in our lives, but this is not the same as facing eternal judgment. Once we have been born again into Jesus Christ, nothing can ever separate us from Him. "For God did not appoint us to wrath," wrote the apostle Paul, "but to obtain salvation through our Lord Jesus Christ, who died for us, that whether we wake or sleep, we should live together with Him" (1 Thessalonians 5:9–10). In another letter, he confidently declared, "I am persuaded that neither death nor life, nor angels nor principalities nor powers, nor things present nor things to come, nor height nor depth, nor any other created thing, shall be able to separate us from the love of God which is in Christ Jesus our Lord" (Romans 8:38–39).

God is always working to draw people to Himself.

God's wrath is a terrible thing to contemplate, as we see in the vivid pictures that David drew. The Lord is angered by injustice and unrighteousness; He resists the proud and turns deviousness back upon itself. His voice thunders and His breath blazes forth, consuming all the wicked deeds of men.

But God takes no delight in pouring out His wrath, and His goal is always to bring the sinner to repentance. His "eyes are on the haughty," David wrote, that He "may bring them down" (2 Samuel 22:28)—that is, that the proud might become humble. God does not look for excuses to destroy people; He looks to draw His children to Himself and make them more like Christ. This does not discount the fact that God's wrath will fall upon those who die apart from Christ but while a person is alive, God's grace and salvation are always available—and the Lord uses every means to draw the sinner to Himself.

Once saved, the Christian is *permanently* saved from God's wrath. Thus, for Christians, God's anger toward sin is always expressed as discipline, intended to make us more like His Son, not to castigate us. The difference between Saul and David is the difference between judgment and discipline. If we will submit to His discipline, we will be conformed to Christ's image: "Now no chastening seems to be joyful for the present, but painful; nevertheless, afterward it yields the peaceable fruit of righteousness to those who have been trained by it" (Hebrews 12:11).

↳ Digging Deeper ↲

5. *What character traits did David describe in these two psalms? What pictures did he use to describe God's wrath? God's grace and mercy?*

6. *What does it mean to "blot out" one's transgressions? Why does God do this? What is required of us?*

7. Why did David say that he had sinned against God alone? Why did he not include Uriah and Bathsheba in the list? What does this teach about the nature of sin?

8. Why did David say, "I was also blameless before Him" (2 Samuel 22:24)? What did he mean? What does this teach about God's view of His people?

⁓ TAKING IT PERSONALLY ⁓

9. Are you a person after God's own heart? What is entailed in that? How can you strengthen that quality this week?

10. Is there any unconfessed sin in your life? Take time right now to confess it before the Lord.

Section 4:

Summary

Notes and Prayer Requests

REVIEWING KEY PRINCIPLES

✎ LOOKING BACK ✎

From the past eleven studies, you have gained an overview of the reign of Israel's great King David. In the process you have met a variety of people whose lives were both good and bad. Together, we have admired David's skillful leadership and been shocked at his profound weaknesses. We have considered Joab, a valiant soldier who was also a treacherous murderer. We saw David mourn over the destruction of his household as he watched young men with great potential suffer tragic deaths. But one theme has remained constant throughout these studies: *God is faithful,* and those who obey Him will grow in faithfulness as well, each capable of becoming a person *after God's own heart.*

Someone who is "after God's own heart" sets the Lord's will above all other considerations. David demonstrated this characteristic even though he also sinned greatly; when he was confronted with his wickedness, he repented immediately and sought to be restored to an open relationship with God. Joab, in contrast, frequently put his own desires ahead of obedience to God, indicative of a man whose heart is not given fully to the Lord.

Here are a few of the major principles we have found in this study guide. There are many more that we don't have room to reiterate, so take some time to review the earlier studies—or better still, to meditate upon the Scripture we have covered. Ask the Holy Spirit to give you wisdom and insight into His Word. He will not refuse.

✎ SOME KEY PRINCIPLES ✎

Division is the devil's tool.

The nation of Israel divided when King Saul died, each half placing their allegiance behind a different heir to the throne. That same division would return later in David's reign, and would ultimately divide Israel into two separate nations. Each time the people were divided, strife and civil war resulted. Abner was forced to fight Asahel, a young man he admired, when the two men should have been fighting side by side against the Philistines.

This is Satan's goal in dividing God's people: if we are busy contending against one another, we won't be doing battle against the forces of darkness. The evil one loves to see

Christians bickering and scratching at one another, and he will do all he can to cause division and contention within the church.

The Lord wants His people to be unified together in one body, focused on serving one another and caring for one another as members of the same body. "Now I plead with you, brethren," wrote the apostle Paul, "by the name of our Lord Jesus Christ, that you all speak the same thing, and that there be no divisions among you, but that you be perfectly joined together in the same mind and in the same judgment. . . . For where there are envy, strife, and divisions among you, are you not carnal and behaving like mere men? For when one says, 'I am of Paul,' and another, 'I am of Apollos,' are you not carnal?" (1 Corinthians 1:10; 3:3–4).

God's dealings with mankind are through His grace, not man's merit.

Saul was king over Israel prior to David, but his entire reign was characterized by pride. He evidently felt that he somehow had merited being king, and that he could order events as he saw fit. This attitude led him into many grievous sins, including attempts to murder David and consulting a witch for guidance instead of God.

David's life, in contrast, was characterized by humility (with a few significant lapses, as we saw in Study 4). As a rule, he recognized that he had no merit in himself that deserved God's favor. God promised to establish his throne forever, and even brought the Messiah into the world through David's descendants—but David always understood that God did these things simply because He chose to, not because David had somehow earned His esteem.

God blesses His people because He loves us and it is His very nature to bless those whom He loves. God forgives us because He chooses to forgive, because His character is forgiving and gracious. No human being can ever earn God's blessings, and no person can ever make atonement for his sins. As Paul wrote, "For by grace you have been saved through faith, and that not of yourselves; it is the gift of God, not of works, lest anyone should boast" (Ephesians 2:8–9).

Fulfill your promises.

David and Jonathan loved one another like brothers, and either would willingly have laid down his life for the other. Jonathan, in fact, did risk his life by protecting David against Saul's murderous plans, risking the wrath of both father and king. The two men swore an oath of friendship, and David promised Jonathan that he would always show kindness to him and his family.

But Jonathan died young, fighting bravely against overwhelming odds with the Philistines. David, on the other hand, became king and had battles of his own to deal with. From the world's perspective, he would have been well within his kingly rights to put Mephibosheth to death, lest he prove a menace to his throne. It would have been more than gracious, in the world's eyes, for David to ignore Mephibosheth and let him live. But David took his oath very seriously; it was not enough merely to let Mephibosheth live—he went beyond that and deliberately showed compassion to Jonathan's son, simply because he had promised to do so.

David was imitating the character of God, who always keeps His promises. God's people, too, should take care to fulfill their word, whether given as a solemn oath (as in marriage vows) or merely a simple promise. To not do so invites divine judgment. In fact, according to James, it is better to not give your word at all than to give it and not keep it: "But above all, my brethren, do not swear, either by heaven or by earth or with any other oath," he wrote. Then, quoting Christ Himself (Matthew 5:37), he added, "But let your 'Yes' be 'Yes,' and your 'No,' 'No,' lest you fall into judgment" (James 5:12).

God's people must view sin from God's perspective.

When David committed adultery, he viewed his actions from man's perspective. His major concern was to prevent other people from knowing what he had done, and this led him to attempt a cover-up. As we have seen already, however, his cover-up led to more sin and further attempts to conceal it.

If David had viewed his sin of adultery from God's point of view, on the other hand, he would have been quick to confess and repent. Man is concerned with what other people will think, but God is interested in how our sin damages our relationship with Him. David was worried about his reputation as king, while God was thinking of his eternal fellowship.

Today, the world tells us that the most important priority is appearances, placing great value on outward show while claiming that there are no eternal consequences for our actions. God, however, is focused on eternity, so He wants His people to see every sin as something that puts distance between them and Him.

Beware of ungodly counsel.

Jonadab saw that Amnon was pining away after a woman, so he offered advice on how to gratify his carnal cravings. And, like most false counselors, he seemed to be well versed in the intrigues of everyone around him, appearing at the most opportune times to give his advice, as he did when David was grieving.

121

He began his counsel to Amnon by suggesting that the young man deceive his father. Amnon should have recognized that Jonadab's advice was ungodly and rejected it outright. Instead, he followed Jonadab's poisonous "wisdom," though he was not compelled to do so.

Today, the world bombards us with ungodly counsel that, like Jonadab's, often sounds wise and expedient, but God's people are called to weigh every teaching against the teachings of Scripture. Godly counsel never advises us to disobey God's commands. Had Amnon considered that, he may actually have succeeded his father on the throne.

Do not be ungrateful.

Ziba had experienced much blessing in his life. He had been entrusted by King Saul to oversee all the king's lands and possessions, a position that gave him great power and authority. It also gave him significant personal wealth, as his own household had grown to be quite large (2 Samuel 9:10). The death of Saul, however, could easily have ruined him—might even have put his own life in danger. But David's generosity toward the house of Saul enabled him to retain his wealth and remain in his position of steward over Mephibosheth's inheritance. Yet Ziba was an opportunist: rather than being grateful for these blessings, he sought to gain still more through treachery and guile.

Mephibosheth, in contrast, recognized that he was entitled only to death. The fact that he was Saul's only remaining heir would have been a death sentence under any other king, yet David had gone beyond merely allowing him to live by inviting him to dine at the king's table every day—a very high honor. Mephibosheth responded to David's kindness with love and loyalty; his grief was quite genuine over David's banishment from Jerusalem, and his joy was evident upon the king's return.

Christians are in the same position as Mephibosheth. We are all sinners, entitled to nothing but the death sentence from a holy and just God. Yet God has gone far beyond merely forgiving us of our sins and commuting the death sentence—He has also made us children of God and heirs with Christ, inviting us to commune with Him freely, both now and through eternity. When we are tempted to think that life owes us more, it is time to take stock of all God has provided to us through His Son. A thankful spirit will protect us from a spirit of ingratitude.

The Lord is eager to bless, not to punish.

David was filled with fear of God's anger when he failed to follow the Lord's prescribed method of carrying the ark, and that fear hindered his ministry. But the Lord was not looking for excuses to display His wrath; He was eager to bless the people and to lead them into righteousness and obedience. He poured out blessings upon the household of Obed-Edom just as He longed to do for the entire nation of Israel.

Our sin can cause us to have an inaccurate perspective of God's character. We can fall into the error of thinking that God is an angry Being who looks for shortcomings and failures in the lives of His people, eager to punish and rebuke them. The truth is just the opposite: the Lord longs to bless His people, and He is always looking for ways to demonstrate His love toward us.

The ultimate example of this is found in Christ. If God had been eager to punish, He might have simply condemned the entire human race to eternal punishment, since that is precisely what our sins deserved. But He sent His own Son expressly to die on the cross to pay the penalty for those sins, enabling us to be restored to fellowship with Him. As David himself wrote, "The LORD is merciful and gracious, slow to anger, and abounding in mercy. He will not always strive with us, nor will He keep His anger forever. He has not dealt with us according to our sins, nor punished us according to our iniquities" (Psalm 103:8–10).

⌁ DIGGING DEEPER ⌁

1. *What are some of the more important things you have learned from 2 Samuel?*

2. *Which of the concepts or principles have you found most encouraging? Which have been most challenging?*

3. *What aspects of "walking with God" are you already doing in your life? Which areas need strengthening?*

4. Of the characters we've studied, which one have you felt the most drawn to? How might you emulate that person in your own life?

ᐦ Taking It Personally ᐦ

5. Have you taken a definite stand for Jesus Christ? Have you accepted His free gift of salvation? If not, why not?

6. What areas of your personal life have been most convicted during this study? What exact things will you do to address these convictions? Be specific.

7. What have you learned about the character of God during this study? How has this insight affected your worship or prayer life?

8. List below the specific things you want to see God do in your life in the coming month. List also the things you intend to change in your own life in that time. Return to this list in one month and hold yourself accountable to fulfill these things.

If you would like to continue in your study of the Old Testament, read the next title in this series, *End of an Era*, or the previous title, *Prophets, Priests, and Kings*.